Brother Azarias

Aristotle and the Christian Church

Brother Azarias

Aristotle and the Christian Church

ISBN/EAN: 9783337005535

Printed in Europe, USA, Canada, Australia, Japan

Cover: Foto ©Thomas Meinert / pixelio.de

More available books at **www.hansebooks.com**

ARISTOTLE

AND THE

CHRISTIAN CHURCH

ARISTOTLE

AND THE

CHRISTIAN CHURCH

AN ESSAY

BY

BROTHER AZARIAS

OF THE BROTHERS OF THE CHRISTIAN SCHOOLS

LONDON

KEGAN PAUL, TRENCH & CO., 1, PATERNOSTER SQUARE

1888

(The rights of translation and of reproduction are reserved.)

PREFACE.

THE present Essay is prepared, by request of the Concord School of Philosophy, as a contribution to its Summer Session of 1887. The Essay proposes to establish two points:

1. Documents not long discovered and only recently availed of, have enabled the Author to place, for the first time, he believes, before the English reader, the true record of the attitude of the Church towards the Aristotelian Philosophy, from its condemnation by the Council of Paris in 1209 to its full recognition by the Legates of Pope Urban V. in 1366. This has been hitherto a vexed question, but ill-understood and ill-explained.

2. The Author has also endeavoured to show the spirit in which the Schoolmen worked, and to prove that the Philosophy evolved by them is as distinct from that of the Lyceum as Saint Peter's is from the Parthenon. Aristotle's influence is there; his terms and his formulas are employed, but the inner spirit and the guiding principle are far different.

In developing these two points, the Author has made no effort to exhaust his subject. He is content to throw out suggestions and indicate lines of thought which the reader may pursue into further details. The subject is no less vast than it is important. The literature which has grown out of it is rich, varied, and extensive. Cardinal Manning, in a letter addressed to the Author upon reading the proof-sheets, shows cause why this importance attaches to the subject. With the permission of His Eminence, the Author quotes from that letter the following passage, which will have all the more weight when it is remembered that His Eminence in early manhood was moulded in the Aristotelian discipline which St. Edmund had introduced into Oxford, and that later on, His Eminence learned to appreciate the depth and grasp and power of St. Thomas:

"The supremacy of Aristotle in the intellectual world of nature, and that of St. Thomas in the illumination of Faith, are the two great lights of natural and supernatural truth. From the time of St. Edmund, who brought the study of Aristotle from Paris to Oxford, the tradition of study at Oxford rested on Aristotle and Faith. Now it has wandered to the world of rationalism which Aristotle and St. Thomas purified.

"Your book will be very useful in recalling students to the world-wide philosophy of the Catholic Church."

The Author sends the Essay forth with the hope and the prayer that it will, in however slight a degree, be found to serve the purpose indicated by His Eminence.

LONDON, *August*, 1887.

CONTENTS.

		PAGE
I.	Attitude of the Church towards Philosophy	1
II.	The Church and her Apologists	7
III.	Aristotle and his Influence	13
IV.	Aristotle in the West	18
V.	Aristotle in the East	26
VI.	Aristotle among the Arabs	33
VII.	Aristotle and the Church	49
VIII.	Aristotle in the University	66
IX.	Limitations of Thought	76
X.	The Spirit in which the Schoolmen worked	85
XI.	Aristotle and the Schoolmen in Metaphysics and Psychology	99
XII.	Aristotle and the Church in Morals	112
XIII.	Conclusion	128
	Appendix	135
	Index	137

ARISTOTLE

AND THE

CHRISTIAN CHURCH.

I.

ATTITUDE OF THE CHURCH TOWARDS PHILOSOPHY.

A PRELIMINARY statement that will prevent grave misconception in the course of the following pages, is this: The Church is not in any sense a School of Philosophy; she is a living, organic body, informed by the Holy Spirit for the regeneration of the world. With this view does she teach definite doctrines, and inculcate definite practices, and, by means of the prayer of ritual and ceremonial and sacramental blessing, impart to men grace and strength to live up to her teachings. Her Divine Founder was of no School; He was bound by no system; He defined not; He gave no syllogistic demonstrations. With a sublime simplicity, in the power of the Divinity alone to assume, He laid down His doctrines, confirmed His disciples, and organized His

Church. Whatever was good and humanizing in the Mosaic law He retained; all that was harsh and hardening He abolished, and taught by precept and example the universal law of Love. And the Church, like the Truth on which she is founded, has ever remained above all systems and all schools. She allows her children, as best they can, in the light of such philosophic truth as they find at hand, to endeavour to explain her doctrines and her dogmas. Being a living organism, she speaks to each age in the language that each age best understands. And so it happens that, in defining and affirming the doctrines of which she is the sacred depository, as against schism or heresy, she from time to time adopts some term or other from the prevailing philosophic school—when that term most clearly expresses her thought. In the Catechism that she places in the hands of the child just arrived at the age of reason, she teaches in philosophical language the nature of the Sacraments that she administers; and in distinguishing between what constitutes their Matter, and what their Form, she is using a nomenclature familiar to the Schools hundreds of years before her Divine Founder breathed into her His sanctifying Spirit.

Thus it is that, under her influence, "doctrines concerning the nature of God, the immortality of the soul, and the duties of men, which the noblest intellects of antiquity could barely grasp, have become the truisms of the village school, the proverbs of the cottage and the alley."[1] All this is to be looked for in a living organism addressing herself, not to one portion of humanity, but to every portion, be it of the learned or the ignorant, of the rich or the poor, of the savage or the civilized. Hers must needs be a teaching and a practice to satisfy intellect as well as heart. She must needs contain within herself a fulness and a wealth of grace to calm the stormy heart, and of truth to bring repose to the restless brain of an Augustine, to satisfy the intellectual cravings of a Novalis and a Frederick Schlegel, and to meet the questionings of the acute intellect of a Cardinal Newman. But if she were not equal to all this, would her Divine Founder ever have spoken of Himself as the Fountain of living waters, at which whoso drinks will never feel thirst?[2] And therefore it is, that as she grows with the growth of the ages, is she found equal to the wants of every age. Whatever there is of the good, or the true, or the beautiful; whatever tends to bring home to a people's heart her sublime teachings; whatever appeals to man's highest reason, and satisfies his noblest aspirations, she absorbs and assimilates and presents for his contemplation, blessed and purified and consecrated as an instrument of holiness. There is no truth too elevated for her grasp; there is no detail too trivial to be

---

[1] Lecky, *History of European Morals*, vol. ii. p. 3.
[2] John iv. 13.

beneath her notice, if it can only avail for the main purpose. Jesus comes to establish a regenerative religion. He takes up His abode amongst that people the most intensely religious upon the face of the earth. He establishes the Christian principle. And an impartial witness to the worth of that principle says of it: "Infinitely greater and more fruitful than Jewish tradition, the Christian principle was large enough to comprise all, and powerful enough to absorb all. . . . . All that speculation conceived of the profound and elevated in metaphysics, all that practical good sense found most certain and most efficacious in morality, Christianity hastened to gather up and make its own."[1]

The disciple whom Jesus loved in an especial manner, and who fully understood the spirit of the New Religion, before recording the sayings and doings of his Master, premised his Gospel with a vindication of the Godhead of Jesus, and with giving, in opposition to the teachings of Philo (circ. B.C. 25 to circ. A.D. 50) and the Alexandrian School, a proper place in Christian philosophy, to the Word, in language as clear, simple, and sublime as

---

[1] Vacherot, *Histoire Critique de l'École d'Alexandrie*, tom. i. pp. 168, 169. The author adds those words, no less true : "On n'a voulu voir le plus souvent dans la philosophie chrétienne que l'origine de toutes les erreurs qui ont infesté l'Église ; on aurait dû y voir également la source de toutes les grandes vérités qui composent la partie supérieure et vraiment métaphysique du Christianisme." Later on we shall have occasion to note a practical application of their truth.

ever dropped from the pen of inspiration. Therein does he establish the co-eternity of the Word with the Father: *In the beginning was the Word, and the Word was with God.* According to Philo, the Word was a mere attribute of God: now the Divine Reason, now the Divine Creative Power, now the child of His wisdom; never God Himself.[1] John identifies the Word with the Godhead, and states His Divine Personality: *And the Word was God . . . In Him was life, and the life was the Light of men. . . . And the Word was made flesh, and dwelt amongst us.*[2] Henceforth in Christian philosophy Jesus shall be known as the Word, bringing to men light and life, regeneration and redemption. This is the touchstone of all systems: *By this is the Spirit of God known. Every spirit, which confesseth that Jesus Christ is come in the flesh, is of God: And every spirit that dissolveth Jesus, is not of God.*[3]

And yet, though an inspired Gospel, in a sublime preamble, dissolves the philosophical myths in which vain imaginings would cloud the Divinity of Jesus, it is not as a system of philosophy competing with other systems that the Church steps upon the world's scene. The trained intellect of a St. Paul contrasting her simple teaching with Hellenic culture, on the one hand, finds it to be foolishness for the Greek; on the other hand, com-

---

[1] Ueberweg, *History of Philosophy*, vol. i. pp. 230, 231.
[2] John i. 1, 4, 14.   [3] 1 John iv. 2, 3.

paring it with Jewish history and Jewish traditions, he calls it a stumbling-block to the Jew.[1] Still, the Gnosticism of the day concentrated all its energies in a desperate struggle to crush out of existence the foolishness and the stumbling-block. St. Paul raises his voice against the false science that has crept into the Church, and cautions Timothy not to allow himself to be ensnared by fables and genealogies without end,[2] and to avoid foolish and unlearned questions, knowing that they beget strifes.[3] We know what havoc this Gnosticism played in the early Church. That the world was the work of a delirious God; that the body was evil in itself; that only an elect few were redeemed, only an elect few were predestined to salvation: such were some of its most pernicious doctrines, which were carried out to their full consequences in all the affairs of social and daily life. Loud and fierce did those winds blow; but the Church calmly abided her hour, and the truth prevailed. So was it with the Alexandrian School, with her strange jumble of doctrine. Hard, indeed, were it for the world to become regenerate upon a syncretism in which attempt was made to reconcile Plato with Aristotle, Chaldaic theurgic rites with Judaic mysticism. It was the last bulwark thrown up by an exhausted and expiring civilization against the encroachments of Christianity. It failed; and the Church continued her mission of regenerating and reconstructing the world.

[1] 1 Cor. i. 23.   [2] 1 Tim. i. 4.   [3] 2 Tim. ii. 23.

II.

THE CHURCH AND HER APOLOGISTS.

THIS attitude of calm reserve in regard to all systems and schools, the Church maintains during the long years that she is establishing and confirming her dominion throughout the world. Her great Apologists defend her, and attempt to show forth the sublimity of her teachings. When they speak well, she approves and blesses; when they say aught contrary to the truths of which she is the faithful custodian, she condemns. Justin Martyr (*d.* 166) is a philosopher of the School of Plato. The sublime doctrines which he imbibed in that School lead him to the threshold of the Church.[1] Grace does the rest, and Justin Martyr becomes one of the most eloquent defenders and expounders of the truths of Christianity.[2] He seals with his blood the conviction that he indites with his pen. He seeks to reconcile the truths of Faith with the highest and noblest truths of philosophy. Throughout his discourses there runs the postulate

[1] *Dialog. c. Tryphone,* cap. ii., iii.   [2] Ibid., cap. viii.

which the Church ever insists upon, that between the dogmas of Faith and the conclusions of reason there can be no contradiction.[1] He tells us that among all men are to be found seeds of truth;[2] that whatever things were spoken with truth are the property of the Christian;[3] that Christian truth is fuller and more Divine than that which has been handed down by sage and poet.[4] Athenagoras had a noble conception both of philosophy and religion, and eloquently did he attempt their reconciliation; but if he relies mainly upon Plato in his plea for Christians,[5] in his proofs for the resurrection of the body, he is more a disciple of Aristotle.[6] Tertullian (165–268) seems to hold Plato and Aristotle in equal abhorrence. "Thanks," he says, "to this simplicity of truth so opposed to the subtlety and vain deceit of philosophy, we cannot possibly have any relish for such perverse opinions."[7] But Tertullian did not escape the censure of the Church

---

[1] *Apologia, I. pro Christianis*, cap. ii.
[2] Ibid., cap. xliv.   [3] Ibid., ii. cap. xiii.
[4] *Apol.*, i. cap. xx. There is extant a work purporting to be a refutation of Aristotle by Justin-Martyr. But it is spurious. It attempts to prove the non-eternity of matter and the immortality of the soul, as against the opposite doctrines stated in the treatises *Physicæ Auscultationis* and *De Cælo*. The Latin version—*Eversio Falsorum Aristotelis Dogmatum, Authore D. Justino Martyre*—bears date Paris, 1552.
[5] *Legatio pro Christianis*, cap. xxiii.
[6] See his reasoning in cap. ii. of his treatise, *De Resurrectione Mortuorum*.
[7] *Adv. Marcion*, lib. v. cap. xix.; *Opp.*, tom. ii. col. 521.

when, in the rashness of his bold and brilliant intellect, he broached doctrines opposed to those in her keeping. It is always dangerous to despise and antagonize aught of good in any of God's creatures.

In a more conciliatory spirit laboured the great philosophers of the Christian Schools of Alexandria. Clement and Origen—both of them great in genius, great in piety, great in the depth and eloquence of their writings—gather into a single focus the rays of truth that they find in all systems, whether of the East or of the West, and attempt a Christian encyclopædia of philosophy and theology, worthy of the Church they would defend and of the noble truths they would explain. Nothing comes amiss to Clement. He sifts, examines, chooses whatever he lays hands upon; whatever he finds good therein he makes his own. "I call him truly learned," he says, "who brings everything to bear on the truth; so that from geometry, and music, and grammar, and philosophy itself, culling what is useful, he guard the Faith against assault. Now, as was said, the athlete is despised who is not furnished for the contest."[1] In this truly eclectic spirit did Clement work. In this truth-loving and truth-searching spirit also did Origen work. He tells us that the Apostles on many points were content with saying that things are; why they are, or how they are, they abstained from making known; leaving to studious men

[1] *Stromaton*, lib. i. cap. ix.; *Opp.*, tom. i. col. 739.

and lovers of Wisdom to investigate these things, clearly in order that those of them most worthy might have a subject of exercise on which to display the fruit of their talents.[1] In so acting the Apostles were carrying out the spirit of the Church.

Later on, when controversy raged fiercely upon the doctrine of the Trinity, the Church raised her voice, and in the Council of Nicæa, A.D. 325, defined that doctrine in terms clear and simple. Forthwith the co-eternity, equality, and consubstantiality of the Father, Son, and Holy Ghost, became a life-giving truth that saved Christendom from the blight of the cold monotheism of Mohamed, or the decayed polytheism of Paganism. This great truth held up for contemplation the Father illuminating humanity by His Word, and sanctifying it by His Holy Spirit. "*We believe in one God the Father Almighty, Maker of all things visible and invisible, and in one Lord Jesus Christ the Son of God . . . begotten, not made, consubstantial with the Father, through Whom all things came into being, both the things in heaven and the things in earth; Who for us men and for our salvation came down and was made flesh . . . and in the Holy Ghost.*"[2] Such are its leading terms. It is only the defining of a religious dogma; but that definition becomes a landmark upon the road of intellectual progress. In

---

[1] *De Principiis*, Introd., § 3.
[2] Hefele, *History of the Christian Councils*, vol. i. p. 294.

the few simple words of the Nicene creed—steering clear of Gnostic reveries and Platonic dreams, of barren monadism and confusing polytheism—we find summed up more than philosophy could invent or imagine concerning the nature of the Godhead. It was the answer of the Church to the attempt of the Neo-Platonists to crush her and set up against her teachings a strange jargon of all systems and all religions. And upon this solid basis was it that St. Augustine nobly refuted their errors, whilst admitting whatever was good in their system.[1]

Inimical as Neo-Platonism was to the Church, the children of the Church took from its teachings whatever they considered good or useful for the clearing up of her doctrines. Thus, the writings of the pseudo-Dionysius, possessing much that is true and beautiful, abound in opinions that read like pages extracted from Plotinus and Proclus.[2] St. Maximus (580–662) prizes them highly, and makes of them a careful paraphrase. John of Damascus invokes their authority. Irish monks fostered the Neo-Platonic philosophy in the West. They were at this time the only Hellenists of Europe, and their Hellenism was that of Alexandria. Whence Alcuin calls Clement the Hibernian and his associates Egyptians. "In going away," he writes to Charlemagne from his monastery in Tours, "I had left Latins

[1] *De Civ. Dei*, viii. 6.
[2] See Vacherot, *Hist. Crit. de l'École d'Alexandrie*, tom. iii. chap. i.

about you; I know not who has replaced them by Egyptians."[1] Through the Greek studies of these monks were the Neo-Platonic traditions handed down. They were Alexandrians in philosophy as well as in mathematics. Finally, Scotus Erigena, a brilliant scholar, the ornament of the Court of Charles the Bald, teaches school in Greek,[2] translates the works of the pseudo-Dionysius into Latin, and disseminates the philosophy of Proclus.[3] Aquinas clinches many an argument with weapons drawn from the Dionysian writings. Later on, in the reaction against the disputations of the Schools, we find a Mysticism, based upon their teachings, spread far and wide; and, under the guidance of Tauler, Henry Suso, and the Society of Friends of God, influence whole sections and peoples. It is also through a disciple of Neo-Platonism that Aristotle begins his sway in the West. Boëthius (470–526) makes his studies in Athens. He brings back with him, among other works, parts of the Aristotelian Logic, with the Introduction of Porphyry. These he gives to the students of the West in elegant translation.

[1] *Epist.* 82, an. 798; Hauréau, *Singularités Historiques et Littéraires*, p. 26.
[2] Gidel, *Nouvelles Etudes sur la Littérature Grecque Moderne*, p. 178.
[3] The writings of Scotus Erigena were condemned in 1220.

III.

ARISTOTLE AND HIS INFLUENCE.

ARISTOTLE will now enter upon a career of conquest and influence far exceeding the conquest and the influence of his great pupil, Alexander. Let us pause a moment at the threshold of his power. Schools and systems rise and flourish and become a thing of history; but centuries, now of neglect, now of undue admiration, having elapsed, Aristotle blooms into perennial freshness long after those who admired or condemned him have passed into oblivion. Certainly, the secret of this influence lies not in elegance of style, nor in glow of expression, nor, as we now possess him, in harmony of arrangement. His language is at this day sometimes obscure, sometimes almost unintelligible, generally severe; with much weariness of spirit is he read, but also with none the less avidity.[1] "The half-understood words of

---

[1] Cicero studied Aristotle in Athens, in the very atmosphere of his writings, and surrounded by all the traditions of the Lyceum, and yet he found the study of him difficult: "Magna animi contentio adhibenda est in explicando Aristotele" (Frag. Hortensius). See J. B. Saint Hilaire, *Met. d'Arist.*, tom. i., Pref., p. ii.

Aristotle have become laws of thought to other ages."[1] Even when he was handed down in imperfect translation and was but ill-understood, his genius, though clouded, remained not without recognition. He was called the Prince of Philosophers;[2] the Master of them that know;[3] the limit and paragon of human intelligence.[4] Among the lesser intellectual lights, veneration for him became a superstition, and no word of his would they dream of disputing. Such over-estimation led to reaction. The pious regarded him as the root of all heresy.[5] The Humanists found the polished pages of Plato more congenial, and accordingly upon Plato expended all their enthusiasm. The Reformers found him too identified with Catholic dogma to subserve their purposes. We know what Luther thought of him: "If Aristotle had not been of flesh, I should not hesitate to affirm him to have been truly a devil."[6] Both Bacon and Descartes, each after his own manner, directed their whole energies towards the overthrow of the Stagyrite in order to prepare the way for their respective systems. The philosophers of the eighteenth century neither under-

---

[1] Jowett, *Politics of Aristotle*, Introd. p. ix.
[2] St. Thomas Aquinas.   [3] Dante.
[4] Averroës.
[5] See the concluding chapter of Postello, in *Eversio Falsorum Aristotelis Dogmatum*, p. 75, *sqq.*
[6] Ueberweg, *Hist. of Phil.*, vol. ii. p. 17. Later on, through the influence of the more conservative Melancthon, his Dialectics were exempt from Luther's general condemnation.

stood nor appreciated him.¹ Diderot calls his philosophy one of the greatest plagues of the human intellect.² The nineteenth century is more just. After having tested many systems of philosophy—after Kant and Hegel and Schopenhauer and Cousin and Mill and Herbert Spencer have spoken—we find the current of thought drifting back once more towards Aristotle. And we are returning with many advantages over his early admirers. We have purer texts. The history of philosophy is better known, and throws light upon many points hitherto but imperfectly understood. The spirit of study at the present day is thoughtful and many-sided. It ignores no element. It recognizes no break. It finds opinions of the present intimately related to ideas in the remotest past. It accepts as a primary principle that in the world of ideas, as in that of society, thoughts are generated, grow, and develop according to laws as rigid as those governing the generation and development of the human body. It postulates as an elementary condition of right-knowing, that in order to apprehend any subject properly, one must search and consider the contributions that have been made to that subject in the past, and, if possible, lay finger upon the germs of the thoughts that are now full-blown. The spirit of study pursued in

---

[1] See J. Barthélemy Saint-Hilaire, *De La Logique d'Aristote*, tom. ii. p. 194.

[2] *Œuvres*, tom. xix. p. 372.

conformity with these principles, must needs appreciate the importance of an intellect that during twenty-odd centuries has been moulding the forms of thought and constructing the grooves in which the trained intellects of civilized Europe should reason.

The genius of Aristotle stands out in strong contrast with that of his great master, Plato. His frame of mind was in many respects diametrically opposite. He lacked the religious fervour of his master. He was emphatically a man of the world, whereas Plato was a recluse. He was wanting in that reverence for antiquity and all belonging to it—the old myths, the old cosmogonies, the old traditions—that lend such a charm to the pages of Plato; and if he does speak of his predecessors, and accept what they handed down, with a certain modesty, it is simply the modesty belonging to every close student who knows his own limitations. Plato was governed by an enthusiasm that lit up his soul and revealed to him the highest and noblest regions of ideal thought and emotion; Aristotle looked at the cold facts of the case, dissected every element of thought and expression with the coolness of the surgeon handling the scalpel, and set down his observations in the dryest and baldest manner.

What were the personal feelings of the Stagyrite towards his great teacher? Were they friendly, or were they antagonistic? We know not. We can only surmise. But, whether Aristotle gave the sense of Plato as he understood that sense; whether he concealed the true meaning of his master's teaching and gave only the literal external rendering thereof; or whether he deliberately, and with malice aforethought, changed and distorted his master's doctrines; or whether, still, he merely took the imperfect expression of them as given by disciples unable to grasp their whole bearing, and answered these with a view simply of making them so many pegs on which to hang his own doctrines: be the explanation what it may, the real position of Aristotle's philosophy in the history of thought is that it stands out from the philosophy of Plato, not as a mere contradiction to that philosophy, but as completing and perfecting it, and supplying its shortcomings. He laid hold of the laws of thought and made of them a science. He separated philosophy from fable and myth and metaphor, and gave it a method and a scientific terminology.[1] He developed the syllogism to a degree of perfection that has left it the admiration of all succeeding thinkers. He taught after-ages how to classify and how to define with accuracy and with method. More than this has he done; but this much suffices to establish his claim upon the appreciation of men for all time.

[1] He himself tells us the φιλόμυθος was also the φιλόσοφος. *Met.*, i. 2, § 4.

IV.

ARISTOTLE IN THE WEST.

The Aristotelian philosophy meanders down the ages in two distinct streams, both welling forth from the Alexandrian School like life-blood from the human heart, to meet and mingle centuries afterwards, in the leavening of intellectual life. We have seen that the Western current set in with Boëthius. He gave students, with his own comments, the treatises of Aristotle on the Categories and, in his own word, that on Interpretation.[1] Therein they learned to distinguish between substance and accident, to consider a subject in regard to its environments of time and place, its quality and quantity, its manner and habit of existence, and the like; they learned to establish the relations of subject and predicate, of affirmation and negation, of the possible and the impossible, of the contingent and the necessary; they learned how to examine words, phrases, and sentences.

---

[1] *De Interpretatione*. It was more generally known as *The Perihermenias*. Under this name St. Thomas comments upon it.

All this was wholesome. It was giving the still untrained intellect of mediæval youth a means, and an example of the highest authority, whereby to fix precision of terms, to classify, to define and divide, and to construct propositions with accuracy. But in addition to all this, Boëthius gave a short treatise of Porphyry (232–304) written as an introduction to the Categories. It has been considered a valuable improvement upon the doctrine of Aristotle. But, in the opening chapter of that little treatise, Porphyry poses a problem which he does not there attempt to solve; which is amongst the most important in the history of philosophy; which is also amongst the most difficult to solve, and upon the solution of which schools and even peoples have quarrelled. It is the threefold problem concerning the nature of genus and species. *Do genus and species subsist, or are they solely mental fabrications? If subsisting, are they corporeal or incorporeal? Finally, do they exist apart from sensible objects, or are they in those objects, forming with them something co-existent?*[1] Such are the questions which Porphyry put and refrained from answering,[2] but which Boëthius threw into the Western brain. Porphyry refrained from their solution then and there, because of their difficulty and because they required

---

[1] *Isagoge*, cap. i.
[2] Porphyry had already given their solution after Plotinus, in the *Enneades*, lib. v.

great research;[1] and yet Porphyry held the traditions of the Lyceum and the Academy, and was furnished in the Alexandrian libraries with all the means of research. But without the philosophical traditions of Athens, and without the means of determining the historical position of the problem; with simply a few definitions and with the instrument of the syllogism, the Schoolmen attacked it with all the rashness and energy that come of great ignorance and great strength. It was an epoch-making problem, but it was prematurely thrown upon the intellectual world of the West. Minds were not sufficiently trained for its profitable discussion. None the less did they grapple with it and fight over it; and in the sparks of light that escaped from that question did they discuss all other questions. "Since the world began to solve the question of Porphyry," says John of Salisbury, "the world has well grown old; more time has been consumed than it has taken the Cæsars to conquer and rule the world; more money has been expended on it than ever was in the treasure of Crœsus."[2]

But, can we say that we are still free from the problem? Are we not constructing all our philosophy upon the one problem underlying that of Porphyry? Have we gotten beyond the problem of knowing? Are

---

[1] Altissimum enim negotium est hujusmodi et majoris egens inquisitionis. *Isagoge*, ibid

[2] *Polycraticus*, lib. vii. cap. xii. col. 664. Edit. Migne.

we not divided into as many rival camps, upon the very same issues under cover of other names as were the Schoolmen? Attempt a solution; at once you lay yourself open to attack and contradiction, and other solutions equally plausible are posited, only in turn to be replaced by others again neither more nor less plausible than your own. Had Boëthius allowed that Introduction of Porphyry to lie buried in the East, what might be the history of thought to day? Would men have devoted more time to observation, to language, to letters? Would national literatures have become more developed? Or did the robust discipline, the strain and struggle of intellect clashing with intellect, and wrestling with a problem that even such giants as Plato and Aristotle could no more place beyond dispute than have Kant or Rosmini been able to do in our own day—did it help to lay deeper the foundations of thought and prepare for later developments? Answer we these questionings how we will, the fact remains that thus the problem took possession of the intellect of Europe and for centuries threw it into a turmoil of controversy not unfrequently carried on with passion and recrimination.

It is needless to enter upon the absorbing work that during those ages occupied the Church in her mission of civilizing the barbarians who invaded and overturned the old Roman culture. Small room was there for philosophy in this work. Small place had it in the intelligence of the child of Nature, just emerging from his woodland home, with his simple habits and his few wants. To teach him the elementary truths of the Christian religion, to subdue the native fierceness of his nature, to accustom him to peaceful pursuits, and above all, to induce him to live up to the Christian standard of morality—this was the primary work of the Church. To this must all else yield. If ever pope understood the spirit of the Church, it was Gregory the Great (550–604). He was a student devoted to his books. But possessing in an eminent degree the Roman genius for administration and organization, he makes all else subservient to this end at a time when administration and organization are most needed. Now, Gregory learns that a bishop gives his time and attention to the teaching of letters, doubtless at the sacrifice of his more imperative duty of administering his diocese and furthering the kingdom of God amongst his people; and forthwith Gregory rebukes him severely for undertaking to teach youths pagan myths when in all probability their souls were famishing for the bread of Christian truth.[1] This rebuke has been misunderstood because the times and the circumstances have been ignored.

But according to times and opportunities we may trace the slow expansion of the mediæval intellect. The work so auspiciously begun by Boëthius is continued

---

[1] *Epistolarum*, lib. xi. 54.

by Cassiodorus (468–562), who in his old age compiles manuals for youths. Isidore of Seville (*d.* 636) keeps up the tradition of learning. The Venerable Beda (673–735) also prepares a compendium of philosophy for his boys. Alcuin (736–804) teaches the Dialectics from some of the treatises of Boëthius and from a compendium of the Categories, which he erroneously attributed to St. Augustine. The doses of Aristotle so far administered to the youth of Western Europe were of a mild character. The only part of his writings known in the ninth century was that on Interpretation as translated by Boëthius.[1] Towards the end of the tenth century, the same author's version of the Categories began to be introduced.[2] The education given was more grammatical than philosophical. The Dialectics taught, dwelt almost exclusively among words. Still, by means of these handbooks is the Aristotelian tradition kept alive.

With the eleventh century a new spirit of study breathes over the face of Western Europe. Larger scope of speculation is exercised. The focus of this new spirit is to be found in the Monastery of Bec, where the sacred fires are kept up by Lanfranc and Anselm. But in proportion as intellectual activity becomes rife, does the spirit of rationalism grow bold. It dictates the unorthodox assertions of a Roscellin. It inspires the restless activity of

[1] Hauréau, *Hist. de la Phil. Schol.*, tom. i. p. 97.
[2] Ibid., *loc. cit.*

an Abélard (1079-1142). Men become possessed of a mania for knowledge, and like Abélard fly hither and thither to every master of reputation, only to find their thirst increasing and their craving more unsatisfied. Abélard is attracted to Laon by the fame of the monk Anselm. He has left on record his impression: "I approached this tree to gather fruit, but I found it sterile, like the fig-tree cursed by the Saviour."[1] Adelard of Bath (*flor.* 1100-1130) drifts first to Tours, then also to Laon; but satisfied, neither with himself nor his teachers, he leaves his pupils and, braving untold perils, travels amongst the Greeks, the Syrians, and the Arabs, bringing back with him doctrines more Platonic than Aristotelian.[2] But during the twelfth century the stream of Peripatetic philosophy swells to larger dimensions. Other books of Aristotle find their way into the West, and are translated, and throw more light upon the Catagories and Predicaments, and give further ground for argument.[3] Peter the Lombard (*d.* 1164) applies Aristotelian principles to theological questions,[4] and constructs the celebrated

---

[1] Hauréau, *Hist. de la Phil. Schol.*, tom. i. *loc. cit.* p. 296.

[2] Jourdain, Am., *Recherches Critiques sur les Traductions d'Aristote*, pp. 97-99, 258-278.

[3] Several translations from the Greek were made during this century. See Jourdain, ibid., cap. ii. James of Venice, for instance, before 1128, translated the Topics, the Prior and Posterior Analytics, and the Elenchos, p. 58.

[4] Not without protest later on. Prior Walter of St. Victor, about 1180, includes him with Abélard, Gilbert, and Peter of Poictiers, as

Book of Sentences, which long after continued to be the manual of all theological students. He was only repeating—and perhaps reproducing—what John of Damascus had done four hundred years previously.[1]

the four labyrinths of France, and accuses all of them of treating with Scholastic levity, being inspired by the Aristotelian spirit, the mysteries of the Trinity and the Incarnation (Du Boulay, *Hist. Univ. Par.*, tom. ii. p. 402 ; Launoy, *De Var. Arist. Hist.*, pp. 49, 50).

[1] The first Latin translation of the *Fons Scientiæ* appeared in 1150. We know what frequent use St. Thomas makes of it in his *Summa*.

V.

ARISTOTLE IN THE EAST.

ANOTHER stream of Aristotelian thought is about commingling with this and adding to the intensity of discussion. It begins at the same Alexandrian source. To trace it thence, through all its windings till it merges with the Boëthian stream, is interesting and instructive. The early Greek Fathers, as a rule, deal more universally with Plato than with Aristotle. The numerous heresies that spring up in the fertile brain of the Greeks and the Syrians, find in the Aristotelian philosophy a basis on which to support their peculiar views; and the more they attach themselves to Aristotle, the more the Catholics become shy of him. Irenæus (140–202), who is profoundly philosophical and versed in all systems, but who makes all subservient to religious truth, accuses Valentinus and his followers of corrupting the candour and simplicity of the Christian Faith by subtleties drawn from Aristotle.[1] In another place, the same Father

---

[1] "Et minutiloquium et subtilitatem circa quæstiones, cum sit Aristotelicam, inferre fidei conantur" (*Contra Hæreses*, lib. ii. cap. xiv. col. 752).

accuses a certain sect of adoring Aristotle as well as the Saviour.[1] Gregory Nazianzen, speaking of various means by which heresy wounds the Church, mentions, among others, the low artifices of the Aristotelian art.[2] Still, when Julian had forbidden Christian masters to teach the Pagan classics, Gregory prepared a series of text-books, among which is an abridgment of the *Organon*.[3] The Dialectics of John of Damascus, which forms the first part of his work called *Source of Science*, epitomizes the Categories and Metaphysics of Aristotle and the Introduction of Porphyry. It rendered good service in its day,[4] and it is still popular.[5] The bishops of a Council of Pontus accentuated the attitude of the orthodox of their day, when in a letter to the Emperor they said: "We speak according to the Fisherman, and not according to Aristotle."[6] Eusebius cites reproaches made against Artemon and Paul of Samosata for holding Aristotle in too great esteem and seeking less the simple language of the Sacred Scriptures than the art of clothing their impiety with syllogisms.[7] The Nestorians cultivated Aristotle with a special fervour.

---

[1] *Adv. Hær.*, lib. i. cap. 25, *in fin.*
[2] *Oratione*, xxvi.; Launoy, *De Varia Aristotelis Fortuna*, p. 29.
[3] Ueberweg, *Hist. of Phil.*, vol. i. p. 403.
[4] Alzog, *Patrology*, p. 619.
[5] Still he taunts the heretics with making Aristotle the thirteenth Apostle (*Contra Jacobitas*, tom. i. col. 1441. Migne edit.).
[6] Launoy, ibid., *Piscatorie non Aristotelice loquimur.*
[7] *Eccl. Hist.*, bk. v. cap. xxvii. p. 417. Edit. Laemmer.

Diodorus of Tarsus, who in his anxiety to escape the errors of Appollinarius, had laid the seed of Nestorianism, wrote a work on the errors that he found in the Physics of the Stagyrite.[1]

But the School of Edessa became a great centre of Aristotelian doctrine, whence it was carried far and wide throughout the East. The story of the fate and the varying fortunes of this School is very instructive. The one first to give it a world-wide reputation was a genius great as a poet, great as an orator, great above all as an educator. His name, for centuries after he had passed from the scene of his labours, possessed a magic spell for the Syrian mind.[2] Bardesanes (b. 154) was a staunch champion of the Church under persecution; but in the latter part of his life he fell away and became known as the last of the Gnostics. His teaching and influence overshadowed the School till about the middle of the third century, when we find its Christian character once more asserted. From its benches went forth St. Lucian, whose Greek version of the Scriptures became as authoritative in Asia Minor as the Latin version of St. Jerome in the West. He founded the celebrated School of Antioch, and modelled it after that of Edessa. Then Edessa enjoyed another brilliant era of about eighty years under the

---

[1] Cave, *Script. Ecclesiast. Hist. Lit.*, vol. i. p. 226.
[2] Cardinal Allemand-Lavigerie, *Essai Historique sur l'École Chrétienne d'Edesse*, p. 24. Paris, 1850.

influence of St. Ephraim (*d.* 378) and his disciples. The writings of Ephraim are regarded as Syriac classics of the purest style. His fervent religious poems merited for him the title of Lyre of the Holy Ghost. The story of his life reads like romance. His early poverty, adventures, and mishaps; his education by his saintly bishop; his exquisite knowledge of his mother-tongue; his teaching it in the school of Nisibus; his flying to Edessa and working in the public baths to make a living; his becoming a monk; the fame of his conferences and commentaries going out; his being called to the chair of Sacred Scriptures in the School of Edessa; his being made deacon in his old age and the wonderful sermons he preached: it is all a life-story that has hallowed Edessa in the heart of every lover of literature.[1] But other influences were soon to change the face of the School of Edessa. Under Ibas, the Nestorian bishop of the place, Cumas and Probus translated from Greek into Syriac the Nestorian writings of Theodore of Mopsuesta and the works of Aristotle.[2]

---

[1] Assemanni gives this short fragment from the Syriac of Benattib: "James of Nisibus established St. Ephraim, teacher of the Syriac language; but after the invasion of the Persians, Ephraim fled to Edessa, where he spent the remainder of his days, and directed a school which continued after his death" (Assemanni, *Bibl. Orient.*, tom. iii. p. ii., *Dissertatio de Syris Nestorianis*, p. 924). Alban Butler, in his *Lives of the Saints*, gives a very indefinite and very colourless account of St. Ephraim.

[2] In this work of translating Aristotle into Syriac Catholics as

Indeed, the School became such a hotbed of heresy that it was scattered, in 489, by the Emperor Zeno; the extensive buildings were demolished, and a Church was built upon the site.[1]

Narses, after having taught Sacred Scriptures for twenty years in Edessa with signal success, removes, in 490, to Nisibus.[2] He there establishes a School to which flock many of his old pupils. A Syriac record speaks of the event in no complimentary terms. "The leprous Narses," says Simeon Beth-Arsam, "established a school in Nisibus."[3] He is an enthusiastic admirer of Aristotle. He has brought the works of the Stagyrite with him. He teaches and expounds them, and his spirit enters into his disciples. His pupil, Abraham of Casca (*flor.* 502), comments upon the Dialectics.[4] The school of Nisibus enjoys a far-reaching reputation for science and letters. We may form some conception of its extent,

---

well as Nestorians took part. Assemanni mentions the fact in these words: "Hinc patet, apud Syros tum Orthodoxos, tum Nestorianos Philosophiam Aristotelicam prius coli cœptam fuisse, quam apud Monophysitas. Versionem Dialecticæ Aristotelis Jacobus Edessenus fecit. Nicolai autem librum de Summa Aristotelicæ Philosophiæ è Græco in Syriacum transtulit Honainus Isaaci filius" (*Bibl. Orient.*, tom. iii. p. 85).

[1] Assemanni, ibid., tom. iii. part ii. p. 926; also tom. iii. part i. p. 2.

[2] Assemanni, *Bibl. Orient.*, tom. iii. p. ii. p. 927.

[3] Ibid., p. 927. We may add that the cognomen of Narses was *Garbana or Leprosus*. See Assemanni, tom. iii. p. 63.

[4] Ibid., p. 154.

when we remember that less than eighty years after its foundation, it was divided into three distinct schools under three eminent masters, and that one of them —Hannan—had eight hundred students.[1] Its fame extended even to Italy. Cassiodorus hears of it; and in his zeal for the revival of learning amongst the Romans, he writes to Pope Agapetus a letter bemoaning the deplorable state of education in Rome, even to the absence of a single good Christian school in the city, and begging of him to bring from Nisibus some of its learned teachers. These were troublous days in the West; the struggle for existence in the midst of war and invasion, from the Franks on one side and Belisarius on the other, absorbed all men's energies; in consequence naught came of the proposal of Cassiodorus. From the School of Nisibus, the works of Aristotle, after other professors had translated them and commented upon them, passed to the School of Bagdad.[2] There Honain (d. 876), and his son Isaac, and his very clever nephew, Hobaish, made them known to the Arabians.[3] The

---

[1] Assemanni, ibid., p. 927.

[2] Brother Athanasius translated the *Isagoge* of Porphyry into Syriac in 645; Bishop James, of Edessa (d. 768), made a version of the *Categories* (Munk, *Mélanges de Philosophie Juive et Arabe*, p. 313).

[3] Honain translated from Greek into Syriac: (1) *A Book of Philosophic Aphorisms;* (2) Commentaries on the *Categories* and the *Perihermenias* of Aristotle. He corrected the Arabic version of the *Posterior Analytics*, translated by Theodore. He, with his

philosophic mind of Arabia was not slow to appreciate them; it found them most congenial to its thinking. It devoured and assimilated them with an avidity that became infectious.

pupils, Isaac, Hobaish, and Surinus, put into Arabic or Syriac the *Posterior Analytics*, the *Metaphysics*, the book on Physics, that on Generation and Corruption, and that on the Soul (Assemanni, *loc. cit.*, pp. 165-169).

VI.

ARISTOTLE AMONG THE ARABS.

The Mussulman Philosophy was not simply that of Aristotle. An undercurrent of Arabian thought flowed around the older system and gave it a special drift and tendency. This also passed over to the Schoolmen, and brought with it problems all its own which they were compelled to face and refute as best they could. It is only by noting the bearings of this current, deep and narrow and strong, that we can understand and appreciate the drift of many an argument and many a proposition in the Philosophy of the Schools. It is the clue to what would otherwise seem enigmatic or irrelevant.

The Arabian is a sterile intellect. It cannot invent; it cannot originate. It has brought to the whole sphere of thought not a single addition that posterity thinks worth preserving. It simply cultivated and transmitted the sciences which it had received from its Syrian Christian masters. Its chief merit, in the estimate of history, is that it preserved and brought back to Europe the current of thought and of study that had been temporarily diverted. True, it made progress in medicine; but medicine it received from Galen; moreover, it is a recognized fact that the chief physicians in the courts of the Califs were Christians. It made progress in algebra; but algebra it received from the Greek Diaphantus. It gave us the Arabian numbers; but these it received from its Hindu kinsfolk. The Arabians were not linguists. Syrians and Jews translated their scientific works either from the Greek, the Syriac, or the Hebrew. They were plain-thinking children of the desert, who, finding themselves masters of cultured races, went to school to them, and received from them whatever knowledge it was within their intellectual capacity to imbibe. Their narrow religious training limited the scope of the subjects upon which they were allowed to receive instruction from strangers. At first their schooling was confined to the study of medicine and the natural sciences. But soon a taste for philosophical speculation grew upon them. Their master, guide, and almost sole authority was Aristotle. It was an authority that monopolized the cultured Mohammedan intellect even to the exclusion of the Korân. Hence the struggle between philosophy and orthodoxy, which raged for centuries and ended only with the triumph of the Korân.

Throughout the contest, the attitude of the popular mind was one of antagonism to all philosophy. Every philosopher was a heretic who had frequently to submit to persecutions and indignities, sometimes from the people, and sometimes from those in high places who courted the popular favour. Every man given to study was a suspect. Al-Kendi, though the friend of the Calif Al-Mamoun, and charged by him with the translation of Aristotle, does not escape the eye of jealousy. He is calumniated and persecuted, and Al-Mótawakkel confiscates his library.[1] The mosques rang with denunciations of Aristotle, Al-Farabi, and especially Avicenna. In Bagdad, in 1150, all the philosophical works from the library of a Kadhi are burnt.[2] In 1192, the operation is repeated upon the works of another philosopher. We are told of a certain Ibn-Habib, of Seville, who is put to death by the Sultan "because it was proved against him that he worked secretly at philosophy."[3]

We read of Avempace that "he was the banner of his age and the phœnix of his time in the philosophical sciences, for which reason he was greatly exposed to the shafts of malice."[4] Ibn-Khakan wrote a severe satire against him, in which he called him a calamity for religion, an affliction for those who are in the good way.[5] The great Ibn-Roschd, after having basked in the sunshine of

---

[1] Munk, *Mélanges de Philosophie Juive et Arabe*, p. 340.
[2] Renan, *Averroës et l'Averroisme*, p. 31. Paris, 1866.
[3] Gayangos, *History of the Mohammedan Dynasties in Spain*, tr. from the Arabian historian Al-Makkari, vol. i. p. 198.
[4] Gayangos, ibid., vol. i. Appendix, p. xii.
[5] Munk, *Mélanges*, p. 385.

court favour for many years, finds himself persecuted at the end of his life, and his works everywhere proscribed.[1] The historian Makrizi sums up the popular feeling against philosophy when he writes: "The theorizings of philosophers have been the cause of more direful evils than can be mentioned to religion among the Mussulmans. Philosophy has served merely to increase the errors of heretics and add to their impiety an additional impiety."[2] The struggle continues during four centuries. At last philosophy falls into utter disrepute; the spirit of study becomes extinct; the Korân triumphs. If the writings of the great intellects of Arabia would be preserved, they must be translated into Hebrew or written in Hebrew characters.[3] Such being the soil, let us now examine the philosophical growth that sprung from it.

From Syria and from Persia did the Mussulman get the first breath of intellectual freedom that inspired him to rebel against the suffocating thraldom of the Korân.[4] There he learned that he was a free and responsible agent. There he was initiated into that mysticism that

[1] Renan, *Averroës et l'Averroisme*, p. 20.
[2] Munk, *loc. cit.*, p. 315.
[3] We may be considered severe. Renan is not less so: "Incapable of transforming herself and of finding room for any element of life, civil and profane, Islamism tore from her bosom every germ of rational culture" (*Averroës et l'Averroisme*, Avert. iii.).
[4] M. F. Ravaisson, *De La Philosophie d'Aristote chez les Arabes*. Comptes Rendus de l'Académie des Sciences Morales et Politiques, tom. v. p. 16. Paris, 1844.

taught intimate union with the Godhead. Both these truths were heretical. But a century has scarcely elapsed since Mohammed imposed the fatalism of the Korân upon his people, when these doctrines begin to be discussed and to divide the faithful into rival camps. Wâcel ben-'Atha (699–748), chased from the school of Hasan because of his unorthodox opinions, reduced for the first time the teachings of the Kadrites, or those believing in freedom of will, to a scientific system. His school held a medium ground between the faithful and the heretics. It endeavoured to reconcile reason with faith. Its fundamental doctrine was the efficacy of reason to discover all man's moral obligations and all truths necessary for salvation, independently of any religious code.[1] The disciples of this school were known as the Motécallamin.[2] Such was the condition of Islamite thought when the writings of Aristotle raised it out of its apathy into intellectual regions, for it, as new and as wonderful as anything revealed by the fabled lamp of Aladdin.

From the Metaphysics of the Grecian philosopher, men drew forth the theory of the eternity of matter and the denial of all human attributes of God in the sense of the Korân. Others wished to reconcile the doctrine

---

[1] Munk, *Mélanges*, p. 311.
[2] They called their science '*Ilm-al-Calâm*, or science of the word. Hence their name.

of creation with this doctrine of absence of all attributes in God. Even God could not create without willing to do so. How overcome the difficulty? By means of a mental fiction. They conceive attributes existing without a substratum. Therefore will may so exist; and this is the will by which God creates.[1] Again, some would deny causality. To account for sequence, they invented the fiction that accidents are things created, positive and independent of any substance of inherence. For instance, I write. In this act, say they, are four accidents created directly for the purpose: that of the will to move the pen, that of the faculty of moving, that of the motion of the hand, and that of the motion of the pen.[2] Childish doctrines these, becoming a people grappling with problems beyond their ken. They held, in opposition to the fatalism of the Korân, that God's providence extends to things universal alone, and not to the singular or the accidental. But in accordance with Gnostic teachings, they invented intermediate worlds and creations that accounted for the actions of the singular and the individual.[3] Their intellectual cravings were fed upon any number of

---

[1] This is the doctrine of the Motazales, Al-Djobbaï and his disciples. Maimonides refutes it (*Guide des Egarés*, edit. Munk, tom. i. p. 445).

[2] This is the doctrine of the Ascharites (Munk, *Mélanges*, p. 326).

[3] However, the Motécallamin would admit of no intermediary between God and His creation (Munk, ibid., p. 324).

spurious works. They had false writings of Pythagoras; they had false writings of Plato; they had false writings of Empedocles, who was a great favourite among them, and in whose name a philosophical sect was established; they had false writings of Aristotle, more orthodox than Aristotle's own.[1] And there was a Jewish tradition to account for this orthodox work. Aristotle, we are told, became converted by Simeon the Just, and renounced his doctrine concerning the eternity of the world, and all other opinions which he had held in contradiction with the doctrines of Moses.[2]

But the problem that overshadowed all others in Arabian philosophy was the problem of knowing. Aristotle is both indefinite and unsatisfactory in his treatment of this problem. How does reason, which is immaterial, think the material? Where is the bond of connection? Aristotle places it in the creative reason. He tells us that reason is a becoming of all things—τῷ πάντα γίνεσθαι—and a making of all things—ὁ δὲ τῷ παντα ποιεῖν.[3] He further explains the difference between this creative reason and the receptive reason: the creative reason is never at rest; it is eternally active; it does not at one time think and at another time not think; it alone is immortal and eternal; it leaves us no memory of this unceasing work of thought because it is unaffected

---

[1] Munk, *Mélanges*, p. 242.   [2] Ibid., p. 249.
[3] *De Anima*, iii. v. § 1.

by its object;[1] the receptive, passive reason is perishable, and can really think nothing without the support of the creative intellect.[2]

The Arabian philosophers forthwith undertook to account for the existence of this mysterious creative intellect. They found the solution in the apocryphal Theology of Aristotle. They read how God, in contemplating His most absolute and true unity, formed the Supreme Creative Intellect.[3] This is first in a series of intelligences from which finally is derived the creative intellect of which Aristotle speaks. The mode of evolution is somewhat in this manner: There are nine celestial spheres.[4] Soul is the principle of their motion. That motion is circular, and supposes the conception of a particular end, and therefore thought or intelligence.[5] This implies desire. The object of desire is the Supreme Intelligence. But the difference in motion is due to difference in desire. Therefore each sphere should have, besides the Supreme Intelligence, an inferior intelligence to regulate its movements. There exist, then, nine other intelligences emanated from the Supreme Intelligence. They are known as separated intelligences.[6] The lowest of these separated intelli-

---

[1] As against the Platonic doctrine of reminiscence.
[2] *De Anima*, iii. v. § 2. [3] *Theologia Ægyptior.*, lib. xiii. cap. vii.
[4] Aristotle, *Metaphysics*, xii. cap. 7, 8.
[5] Cf. Aristotle, *De Cælo*, II. xii. § 3.
[6] See St. Thomas, *De Substantiis Separatis*, cap. ii. *Opp.*, tom. xvi. p. 184.

gences which presides over the motions of the sphere nearest us—the moon—is the active intelligence by whose influence the passive or material—*hylic*—intellect within us is made active, and becomes the intellect in act. When it comes to be always in act, it is known as the Acquired or Emanated Intellect. To attain to this state is the end of all striving after perfection.[1]

In this manner have Arabian philosophers given the creative intellect a local habitation and a name. This creative intellect they conceived as the sole intellect of humanity, into which all others are merged. "The soul," says Averroës, "is not divided up according to the number of individuals; it is one and the same in Socrates and in Plato; the intellect has no individuality; individuation comes only from sensibility."[2] Did Averroës or any of the Arabian philosophers mean by this creative intellect "a living and permanent humanity?"[3] The very genesis of the intellect in Arabian philosophy which we have given, is in itself sufficient answer. This proves it to be a thing apart from humanity—a distinct creation—to the level

---

[1] See Munk, *Mélanges*, p. 332; also Ravaisson, *Métaphysique d'Aristote*, tom. ii. pp. 542 *sqq*.

[2] *Destr. Destr.*, part ii. disput. ii. fol. 349. See Renan, *Averroës et l'Averroisme*, p. 155.

[3] "*Une humanité vivante et permanente*, tel semble donc être le sens de la théorie averoïstique de l'unité de l'intellect" (Renan, *loc. cit.*, p. 138).

of which a favoured few may attain, and this is all. It is easy and convenient to see the fictions of the present in those of the past.[1]

We can only glance at the names of those Arabian philosophers, whose impress may be traced in the philosophy of the Schools. Al-Farabi (*d.* 950), was one of the great lights of Arabian philosophy. It is noteworthy that he studied under a Christian teacher, John Bar-Gilân. Maimonides says that "all he composed, and specially his work on the principles of things, is of the pure flour of the wheat."[2] But Ibn-Tofaïl finds in his works many contradictions. He taught that there was no happiness for the large majority of men beyond that of the present life. That man should become a separate substance in another life, he called old women's tales.[3] The Supreme Good is attainable only by those possessed of perfect intellectual organizations and every way apt to receive the impression of the active intellect. But his commentaries upon the Logic were quoted with approval by the Schoolmen; William of Auvergne, Albert the Great, and Vincent of Beauvais made frequent use of them. "He opened," says Hauréau, "to

---

[1] Attributing the Positivism of Comte to Averroës, has been well characterized as a distortion of historical truth and a gratuitous lending to the past the inventions of the present (Jourdain, *La Philosophie de S. Thomas*, tom. ii. p. 393).

[2] Munk, *Mélanges*, p. 344.

[3] Ibid., p. 346. Averroës attributes to him the expression.

our Scholastic doctors, as logician, ways which Abélard had never imagined."[1]

Ibn-Sina—Avicenna—(980–1037), was the greatest medical authority among the Arabians. He made his studies under a Christian physician, 'Isa ben-Ya'hya. In the domain of philosophy he is no less eminent. "He can be considered," says Munk, "as the greatest representative of the Peripateticism of the Middle Ages."[2] He gave Albert the Great the model of his commentaries upon Aristotle. His division of the faculties of the soul is that which has been adopted by nearly all mediæval and modern philosophers. His distinction of the animal faculty by which beasts form a judgment—*vis æstimativa*—has been accepted in Scholastic nomenclature as a permanent contribution to philosophical science.[3] But though Avicenna in his endeavour to be conservative had made many concessions to the Korân, he still found but small favour at the hands of his brethren.

Al-Gazali (1058–1111), was known as "the proof of Islamism and the ornament of religion." His was an intensely religious nature which received no satisfaction from any of the philosophical systems of his day. After

---

[1] *Hist. de la Phil. Schol.*, tom. ii. p. 22.
[2] *Mélanges*, p. 366.
[3] St. Thomas adopts it in his great *Summa*, I. i. quæst, lxxix. Art. 4. c. St. Thomas here reduces the five interior sensitive powers of Avicenna to four, by identifying the imaginative with that of fantasy.

examining them all, he found himself landed in scepticism. He distrusted his senses; he distrusted his intellectual faculties. "Are we sure," he asks, "that there will not be another state for us which will be to our waking-mood what our waking-mood now is to our sleeping-mood, so that on arriving at this new state, we should be forced to acknowledge that what we had believed true by means of our reason was but a dream without any reality?"[1] A question this, which is still asked and answered, now affirmatively, now negatively, according to individual bias and prejudice.[2] He grew sceptical of reason, only to throw himself into the arms of religion with all the greater fervour. In the mysticism of the Sûfis were the yearnings of his soul satisfied.[3] The writings and the influence of Al-Gazali extinguished the philosophical spirit in the East. It took its flight into Spain.

Ibn-Badjà—Avempace—(1090-1138), domesticated Arabian philosophy upon Spanish soil. We have already seen how his brilliant talents made him enemies. He

---

[1] *Treatise of Saving the Wandering and Enlightening the Just*, chap. ii., tr. Schmoelders, p. 22.

[2] One of the more recent affirmative answers, purporting to be on a scientific basis, is the *Unseen Universe*. Therein the authors seek to establish a continuity of physical as well as spiritual life beyond the present.

[3] To discuss the Sûfis is beyond the scope of this Essay. Mr. W. S. Lilly has a very good account of them in his *Ancient Religion and Modern Thought*, pp. 162-187.

died comparatively young, but not before he had laid his impress upon his age. He it was who first developed the all-absorbing doctrine of the unity of souls. He also attempted to show how the soul may raise itself up to union with the active intellect.[1]

Ibn-Tofaïl—Abubacer—(1100-1185), was more successful over the same problem. Upon a groundwork of fiction he goes to show that there is no contradiction between the truths of religion and those of science. The hero of his story[2] is born and raised away from society, and by the unaided light of reason, arrives at mystical union with the Godhead.[3] He meets another solitary, who has reached the same point from prayer and meditation upon the Korân. They compare notes and find that upon all essential truths they are of one accord. Hayy, in the first flush of his joy, is desirous of announcing this discovery to his fellow-men. The solitary, who has been among men and knows the world, would dissuade his companion from the enterprise; but to no purpose. They both set out together. Hayy is well received at first; but when he begins to explain his philosophy he is given the cold shoulder. Finding his task unappreciated, he leaves in disgust, and with his

---

[1] Munk, *Mélanges*, pp. 409, 410.
[2] *'Hayy ibn-Yakdhân*, The Living One, Son of the Vigilant.
[3] Of course, intellectual development away from all social intercourse, is, in the nature of things, an impossibility.

companion returns to a life of severity and contemplation.[1] Abubacer was thus expressing the strong popular prejudice against the purest doctrine imparted with the purest intentions when presented under the name of philosophy. But his influence upon Scholasticism was of an indirect nature.

Ibn-Roschd—Averroës—(1126–1198), was patronized and encouraged by Abubacer, who has been called the artisan of his fortunes. He was the Arabian philosopher whose influence was most profoundly impressed upon Scholasticism. Coming into immediate contact and relation with the great men of his day, he absorbed all the learning and spirit of Arabian science. His love for philosophy grew into a passion and a species of religion. "The only religion for philosophers," he said, "is to make profound study of whatever exists; for we can render unto God no more sublime worship than that of knowing His works, which causes us to know Himself in all His reality."[2] His love and admiration for Aristotle knew no bounds. "This man," he says, "has been the rule of Nature and a model in which she seeks to express the type of the last perfection."[3] He epitomized Aristotle; he paraphrased Aristotle; he commented

---

[1] Apud Munk, *Mélanges*, p. 417.
[2] Munk, *Mélanges*, p. 456 note. See also the account of Ibn-Roschd, by Abú Merwân Albâjí, quoted by Gayangos, *Hist. Moham. Dyn.*, vol. i. Appendix, pp. xvii.–xxvii.
[3] Comment., *De Anima*, l. iii.

upon Aristotle. These three operations were known as his three commentaries. He was called emphatically the Commentator. St. Thomas learned and followed his method. We are told by his biographer that it was a novel and peculiar one.[1] Like Averroës,[2] St. Thomas did not know the language of Aristotle.[3] But he got Brother William of Moerbek to make translations directly from the Greek.[4] He procured other versions also from the Greek. These he compared and collated. With a reverence bordering upon veneration,[5] and after the manner of the great commentary of Averroës, he studied the Master word for word and line for line. Note the caution with which he proceeds. Here he explains a passage; there he refutes; in another place he attempts to impose an orthodox sense upon what, at first reading, would seem opposed to the Christian spirit.[6]

---

[1] Tolomæus, *Hist. Eccl.*, lib. xxii. c. xxiv. p. 1154.

[2] Neither Averroës, nor perhaps any Spanish Mussulman, knew Greek (Renan, *Averroës et l'Averroisme*, p. 49).

[3] St. Thomas ne possédait ni l'arabe ne le grec (C. Jourdain, *La Philosophie de S. Thomas*, tom. i. p. 82). This statement does not preclude his having a knowledge of the grammar of the Greek language, for there are traces of such knowledge in his writings.

[4] Tocco. Vita. S. Thom. in *Acta Sanctorum*.

[5] See the Introduction to his Commentary upon the Ethics.

[6] Munk, after Buhle and others, tells us that both Albert and St. Thomas studied Aristotle in the Latin versions made from the Hebrew (*Mélanges*, p. 335). Their first readings of Aristotle may have been from such versions. But St. Thomas used only versions made from the Greek in his commentaries. Jourdain tells us that

Still, for two centuries the great Commentator continues to overshadow the Schools. He is quoted, commented, and refuted. Through him all the errors of Arabian philosophy are transplanted within the very shadow of the Church, and together with those of Aristotle, produce a plentiful harvest of disputes, criminations and un-Christian doctrines. It will be our task to trace their growth and influence through the varying fortunes of the Master Mind of both Christian and Arab.

he frequently cites and compares two such versions. The commentary upon the Metaphysics shows that three distinct versions from the Greek were used. Jourdain refers to no less than fifteen instances as proof. And yet Munk gives Jourdain as his authority for saying that St. Thomas studied Aristotle in Latin versions made from the Hebrew. See Jourdain, *Recherches Critiques sur les Traductions d'Aristote*, pp. 40, 41.

VII.

ARISTOTLE AND THE CHURCH.

FROM the Arabian schools the Peripatetic infection spread to Christian schools and Christian cloisters. Raymond, Archbishop of Toledo and High Chancellor of Castile, established an academy for the translation of the Arabian commentators. "Each day," says Hauréau, "increased the number of books received by the School of Paris from the Academy of Toledo; each day revealed some new science."[1] Translations, both of Aristotle and his commentators, were made from the Arabic into a jargon almost unintelligible and frequently misleading. The translator, in his haste to supply the eager demand, stopped not to enlighten himself upon the meaning of special words and even whole phrases, but transcribed the Arabic terms instead of their Latin equivalents.[2]

---

[1] *Histoire de la Philosophie Scholastique*, tom. ii. p. 62.

[2] Here is a specimen from the Poetics by Hermann: "Inuarikin terra alkanarnihy, stediei et baraki et castrum munitum destendedya descenderunt adenkirati ubi descendit super eos aqua Euphratis veniens de Euetin." And yet Hermann's translations were widely read. See Renan, *Averroës et l'Averroisme*, p. 215.

The doctrine that Averroës gave out as coming from Aristotle, bore to the real doctrine of the Stagyrite as much resemblance as the Alhambra bore to the Parthenon. Nor need this surprise. Hard indeed would it be to preserve unchanged doctrine first passing out of the original Greek through the phrasings of a Syrian mind; thence transferred to the phrasings of an Arabian mind; thence again put into the phrasings of a Western mind in such Latin terms as it might command. Harder still would it be for an Arabian commentator, with his peculiar bias of mind, to grasp all the delicate shades of meaning, difference, and distinction, in which the acute Greek intellect was so much at home, especially after those shades had been travestied in so many renderings.[1] In spite of these difficulties, students and masters blindly accepted and drank in with equal avidity the true and the false. They became intoxicated with the new doctrines. They grew bold, troublesome, and violently disputatious. "Their tongues," in the expressive words of John of Salisbury, "have become torches of war."[2] It is the spirit of rationalism that, from various sources, without collusion, each independently of the other, is inundating the

---

[1] Renan says of the Commentaries of Averroës: "The printed editions of his works are a Latin translation of a Hebrew translation of a commentary made upon an Arabic translation of a Syriac translation of a Greek text" (*Averroës et l'Averroisme*, p. 52).

[2] *Epist.*, 60.

University of Paris. There are strange words heard from the teacher's chair. There are mysterious whisperings carried on behind many a barred door and in many a secret corner, of wonderful social and religious changes about to take place; of the inadequacy and inefficiency of the old order; of the inauguration of a new order and a new gospel. It is written and repeated in the name of a saintly monk that "towards the year 1200 of the Incarnation of Our Lord, the spirit of life having gone out of the two Testaments, the Eternal Gospel was born."[1] Amaury of Bennes (*d.* 1207) broaches a most un-Christian doctrine. He teaches a threefold incarnation: that of the Father in Abraham; that of the Son in Jesus Christ; that of the Holy Ghost in the chosen spirits of the day. He gathers around him disciples who possess a body of secret doctrines and practices. Believing themselves the incarnation of the Holy Ghost, they fancy themselves above sin and regard every passion as lawful.[2] Sometimes the spirit of unbelief breaks loose and is heard aloud; as when Simon of Tournay, after a powerful discourse that had made a strong impression,

---

[1] *Liber Introductorius*, a book made up of extracts attributed to Joachim of Calabria. Quoted by J. V. Le Clerc in *Histoire Litteraire de la France*, tom. xxiv. p. 113. Renan attributes its compilation to the Franciscan, Gerard, of Borgo San-Donnino. See *Revue des Deux Mondes*, tom. 64, p. 111, 1866.

[2] See an account of them by Cæsar of Heisterbach, *Illustrium Miraculorum et Historiarum Mirabilium*, lib. v. cap. xxii. pp. 291-294. Amaury drew largely upon Scotus Erigena for his tenets.

exclaimed in the pride of his heart, that greatly as he had exalted and confirmed the law of Christ, he could be still more effective in destroying it, if he so minded.[1] David of Dinant finds in the pseudo-Aristotle and his Arabian commentators a scientific basis upon which to ground doctrines that embody this rationalistic spirit. "All things are one, for whatever is, is God:" so speaks, in the rashness of youth, his disciple Bernard the Sub-Deacon.[2] Another says: "Hitherto the Son operated; but henceforth to the end of the world it is the Holy Ghost who shall operate."[3] These were among the fundamental doctrines of the new sect. The bishops of France became alarmed at the ravages it was making among their flocks. Not only had it taken possession of the novelty-seeking student; it was found that learned clerics and venerable priests were ardent propagators of the new doctrine. Practical and wealthy men of business, like the goldsmith William D'Aire, were among the most active workers in its behalf. In

[1] Matthew of Paris, *Chronica Majora*, p. 477, Rolls Series, Ad. An., 1201. Thomas of Cantapré attributes the famous blasphemy of "the three Impostors" to Simon of Tournay.

[2] Omnia unum, quia quicquid est, est Deus (Acts of 1210.) Given in Martene and Durand, *Thesaurus Novus Anecdotorum*, tom. iv. col. 163. There is nothing in the genuine works of Aristotle to justify this pantheistic position. Everywhere in his writings is the distinction clearly drawn between God and Nature.

[3] "Filius usque nunc operatus est, sed Spiritus Sanctus ex hoc nunc usque ad mundi consummationem inchoat operari" (ibid., col. 164).

1209 the Provincial Council of Paris condemned the teachings of Amaury and David, and with them the Aristotelian books on which their doctrines were supposed to be based; it forbade in the University all further reading of the Natural Philosophy and commentaries thereon, in private as well as in public.[1]

This decree is of primary importance. Paris was then, and continued to be for centuries afterwards, the great intellectual centre of Europe. The University shared with the Empire and the Papacy the controlling influence over the civilization of the West. "The University of Paris," says Mr. Bass Mullinger, "throughout the thirteenth century, well-nigh monopolized the interest of the learned in Europe. Thither thought and speculation appeared irresistibly attracted; it was there that the new orders fought the decisive battle for place and power; that new forms of scepticism rose in rapid succession, and heresies of varying moment riveted the watchful eye of Rome; that anarchy most often triumphed, and flagrant vices most prevailed; and it was from this seething centre that those influences went forth which predominated in the contemporary history of

---

[1] "Quaternuli magistri David de Dinant, infra natale Episcopo Parisiensi afferantur et comburantur, nec libri Aristotelis de naturali philosophia, nec commenta legantur Parisius publicè vel secreto" (*Thesaurus Novus Anecdotorum*, tom. iv. col. 166). The Acts of the Council of 1209 are not given in full in Labbé or in Hardouin, but they are to be found in the *Thesaurus* of Martene and Durand, *loc. cit.*

Oxford and Cambridge."[1] The decree emphasizes the beginning of a long struggle for existence, upon which Aristotle is now entering, at the threshold of the most active and the most momentous period in the whole history of mediæval thought. In considering the attitude of the Church towards the Stagyrite in the varying phases of his fortune during the following two centuries, we find ourselves constructing one of the most delicate and critical chapters in the annals of the human intellect. It is a subject that has been ill-understood. Enemies of the Church have misrepresented her action in the matter; her friends have indulged in lame excuses and abject apologies for which she has neither recognition nor thanks. A simple statement of facts from documents which it is our privilege to use, will show that both aspersion and apology are uncalled for.

The Aristotelian books condemned by the Provincial Council of 1209, may have been, and in all probability were, distorted editions and epitomes of the Stagyrite, rendered and compiled from Arabian sources. We can safely say that none others could have been in general use so early in the century.[2] Moreover, the same

---

[1] *University of Cambridge from the earliest Times to* 1535, p. 132.
[2] This is the opinion of Am. Jourdain (*Recherches Critiques sur les Traductions d'Aristote*, chap. v. pp. 187-196). Renan is of the same opinion: "Ce qui reste indubitable, c'est que le concile de 1209 frappa l'Aristote arabe, traduit de l'arabe, expliqué par des Arabes" (*Averroës et l'Averroisme*, p. 221). Hauréau, on the con-

spurious works that we have seen influence the Arabian philosophy, were at this period in circulation among the Schoolmen, and in the name of Aristotle introduced Neo-Platonic principles.[1] These also contributed to throw the philosopher in bad odour. However, the decree seems soon to have practically fallen into disuse. This may easily be accounted for.

The beginning of the thirteenth century was a critical period in the history of the University of Paris. The relations between the ecclesiastical authorities on the one hand, and on the other, between the masters and students, were straining more and more to their utmost tension. Out of the frequent quarrels of those days grew the organic constitutional existence of the University as a body. Pope Innocent III. (*d.* 1216) had made his studies in Paris. He realized all the wants of the University; he took the deepest interest in its affairs; by gradually strengthening the hands of masters and

trary, thinks the texts might have been genuine translations directly from the Greek (*Histoire de la Philosophie Scholastique*, tom. ii. pp. 100–105). Roger Bacon says expressly that the causes of the censure were false doctrines " and many passages erroneously translated." See Emile Charles, *Roger Bacon*, p. 412; see also ibid., p. 314.

[1] See an analysis both of the *Theologia*, of which we have already spoken, and the *De Causis*, in Vacherot, *Histoire Critique de l'Ecole d'Alexandrie*, tom. iii. chap. ii. pp. 85-100. The book *De Mundo* is also of the same apocryphal character. It is, by the consensus of critics, attributed to Apuleius (114-190). See J. Barthélemy St. Hilaire, *Météorologie d'Aristote*, Dissert., p. xlii.

students, whilst weakening those of the Chancellor, he inaugurated the work of organization that was completed under Gregory IX. Indeed, the University had grown far and away beyond the controlling power of any one man, however competent.[1] In such a state of affairs it was difficult to enforce any decree. Then again, in the rivalry of schools and masters is to be found another reason why the decree was at most only partially obeyed. Aristotle may not be taught in public under the shadow of Notre Dame; but who can account for the Rue de Fouarre and its dependent schools? Confusion prevailed; the conscientious were scandalized; the less scrupulous defied authority and read Aristotle sometimes openly, more frequently in secret. Innocent III., in 1215, enjoins upon Robert of Courçon, Papal Legate to Paris, to use his utmost endeavour to give better direction to studies in the University, and to remove those occasions of scandal and of error, which are no less pernicious to religion than to science. Robert takes into his counsel many good and learned men. Again do they find that Aristotle is not only read, but that he is made the source whence flow the errors then rife. Again do they condemn his Physics; also his Metaphysics, and all compendiums of them. But the statute of Robert permits the

[1] See *The English Historical Review*, Oct., 1886, Art., "The Origines of the University of Paris," by the Rev. H. Rashdell, pp. 664–667. About 1240 the University seems to have attained full organization.

Dialectics, both ancient and new, the Ethics, and four books of the Topics.[1]

The statute removes the forbidden books from the lecture-hall; but the forbidden books are neither neglected nor forgotten. They are again quietly resumed. The intellectual craving of the day for Aristotle—especially for the prohibited books—will be satisfied with no other food. Doctrinal innovations begin to multiply. Masters quarrel with masters, and in their war of words descend to the greatest puerilities. Philip de Grève, a stern and able chancellor of the University at this time, exclaims:[2] "We have made children of ourselves. . . . We have made of ourselves a laughing-stock to laymen. . . . Master is pitted against master, each gnawing away at the other."[3] And in a sermon preached about 1225, he thus alludes to the influx of rationalism that threatens to overwhelm all study: " The torrents have

---

[1] Launoy, *De Var. Arist. Fortuna*, p. 69.

[2] In 1219, in a difficulty between himself and the Masters, he excommunicated them and imprisoned some, in the absence of the bishop, who was at the time in the Holy Land (Du Boulay, *Hist. Univ. Parisiensis*, tom. iii. p. 93 *sqq.*).

[3] The whole passage is too characteristic and too vivid to be omitted. "Pueri facti sumus, qui nihil aliud facimus nisi pugnam gallorum. Unde rediculum facti sumus laicorum. Gallus insurgit contra gallum et cristatur contra eum, et sibi commanducant cristas, et effundunt viscera, et sese cruentant: sic hodie magister contra magistrum et sese ad invicem corrodunt" (Sermo in Domin. prima in Adv. Domini, *Notices et Extraits des Manuscrits*, tom. xxi. 2ième partie, p. 193).

destroyed nearly all our city; pouring themselves out upon the great sea of doctrine, they have disturbed its waves, hitherto so pure and calm. But as it is wisdom to retreat before the army of death in order to save life, so should we act in these times; it is our only plan to take shelter from the torrent and await its passing over. Though violent and rapid, its waters are only transitory."[1] The Chancellor is bearing witness, in his official capacity, to the power and influence of the innovators. With increasing numbers they grow bolder. No longer confining themselves to the theses which they were engaged to teach or defend, they attack the doctrines, the dogmas, the sacraments, and the mysteries of the Church. There is no subject too sacred for them. The highest and most mysterious truths of religion they attempt to bring within the grasp of their limited understanding. This state of affairs is brought to the notice of the Holy See.

The Chair of Peter was at this time occupied by a man venerable in years—he was then over eighty—but with the wisdom and ripe experience of old age he combined a vigour and an activity rarely to be surpassed in youth. He was the patron of learning and the friend of learned men. He was alive to all the wants of the age. He knew the worth of Aristotle; but he must keep intact the Faith. He must compel speculation to remain upon her own domain. Accordingly, in 1228 Gregory IX.

---

[1] *Notices des MSS.*, pp. 189, 190.

addresses a brief to the Faculty of Theology, rebuking the audacity of those professors who dare to introduce into matters of Faith the opinions of philosophers, especially of naturalists, and who, abandoning the safe doctrines of the Fathers of the Church, endeavour to explain revealed truths by the false and worldly science of those authors. He deplores the evils that have already resulted, and forebodes worse, from this bold manner of treating sacred sciences. He exhorts them no longer to obscure the purity of theology with those opinions, no longer to infect and corrupt the word of God.[1] No name is mentioned in this brief. None was needed. Aristotle was the naturalist who was intruding upon the domain of Faith—Aristotle and his commentators. So was it taken in Paris; but was it so understood in Rome? We think not. We think that Gregory knew the character of the corrupted or suppositious texts then in use. Might it not be that he had learned to distinguish between these and the real Aristotle from his brilliant friend Michael Scott? At this very time Michael was translating Aristotle. It is only the previous year that Gregory, in a letter to Stephen Langton, mentions him in the highest terms as a beloved son who from boyhood up had been ardently devoted to letters and science, who was already well versed in the Arabic, Latin, and Hebrew languages, and who still sought to

[1] Raynaud, *Ad. Annales Baronii*, tom. i. § xxx.-xxxi. pp. 615, 616. Lucæ, 1747.

continue to build upon the foundations laid.[1] In all probability Michael Scott was at that very time in Rome.

Seldom was the University in such commotion as at this period. The masters and the ecclesiastical authorities—the Bishop, the Chapter and the Chancellor—quarrel over rights and privileges. The schools suffer.

[1] Novisti siquidem quod dilectus filius magister Michael Scotus a puero inardescens amore scientiæ litteralis, postpositis omnibus, illam studio continuato quæsivit et in fundamento artium gloriosas superedificans facultates decora se structura munivit, nec contentus littera tantum erudiri latina, et in ea melius formaretur, hebraicæ ac arabicæ insudavit laudabiliter et profecit et sic doctus in singulis grata diversarum varietate nitescit (*Bulletin des Comités Historiques*, 1849–50, tom. ii. p. 255). The letter bears the date of April 28, 1227. It is written in order to remind the Archbishop of Canterbury that the proceeds of a certain benefice within his jurisdiction were reserved for Michael Scott by Honorius III., and that Gregory desires them to be continued in the same channel. "Thus," remarks the editor of this important letter, "in Scotch legend Michael Scott is the companion of demons; in history he is a client of the Pope," and, we may add, the beneficiary of another. It is difficult to reconstruct the life of Michael Scott. Born about 1190; as early as 1217 he began putting out translations of the Arabian commentators; about this time he passed over from Toledo to the court of Frederick; his sojourn there was not more than ten years; in all probability he was in Rome about 1227; he afterwards resided and taught in Paris; about 1230 he began to issue translations of Aristotle—one is dedicated to Gregory's friend Stephen of Provins; another MS. of his bears date of 1241. Some censure passed upon his writings by Albert the Great, and some praise and some abuse from Roger Bacon: this is all that is authentic of Michael Scott. Even this much escaped the notice of the writer of the very indefinite article on him in the *Encyclopædia Britannica*.

The mediation of the Pope is invoked by the masters against the Chancellor and the Bishop. At the same time Aristotle continues to press for recognition. Neither masters nor students are satisfied. If the religious teaching orders are to hold their own in the schools, they must be able to reply at least to the objections drawn from the condemned books and prepare their pupils to refute them. If they cannot teach Aristotle as they now possess him, why not prepare an expurgated text? This is the next suggestion that we find hinted at. It comes to us through Pope Gregory IX. In a Bull bearing date of April 13, 1231, after pronouncing upon the recent issues between the authorities and the masters and students, he once more forbids the condemned books to be read; but he adds the limiting clause that the prohibition shall last only till the books shall have been examined and purged of every suspicion of error.[1] Nor does he delay long before appointing a commission to examine and correct them. He has no difficulty in finding competent men.

There is William of Auxerre, the Archdeacon of Beauvais. His commentaries on the Book of Sentences, show him to be a profound theologian, an acute philosopher, and saturated with Aristotle. He has left an indelible impress upon Catholic theology. In his work is first

[1] Launoy, *De Var. Arist. Fortuna*, p. 59; Du Boulay, *Hist. Univ. Par.*, tom. iii. p. 140.

found fully stated the Aristotelian doctrine of Matter and Form as applied to the sacraments of the Church.[1] The Pontiff learned to appreciate his wisdom and intellectual capacity when, in 1229, William accompanied his bishop to Rome. And, therefore, His Holiness some time previously invited him with others to discuss the educational reforms so urgently called for in the University of Paris.[2] William at this time held a chair in the University. Whilst in Rome, calumnies had been spread abroad concerning him, in consequence of which the Chancellor and ecclesiastical authorities were disposed to deprive him of his chair; so His Holiness wrote to the King, beseeching him to restore William and another[3] to their positions; this he backed up with a missive in almost similar words commending them to the Queen, and begging her to use her influence in their behalf.[4] No stronger proof than this can we have of the esteem in which Gregory held William

---

[1] Juenin, *Commentarius de Sacramentis*, Dissert i. cap. ii. p. 6, Venetiis, 1761. See *Catholic Dictionary*, by Addis and Arnold, Art. "Sacraments;" also Wetzer and Welte, *Kirchen-Lexicon*, on the same subject.

[2] "Cæterum cum iidem Magistri pro Reformatione studii ad Sedem Apostolicam personaliter laborantes honorem Regis et Regni tractarent" (Extract from letter to King Louis IX. *apud* Du Boulay, *Hist. Univ. Par.*, tom. iii. p. 145).

[3] Geoffrey of Poictiers.

[4] Both letters are to be found in Du Boulay, *Hist. Univ. Par.*, tom. iii. p. 145.

of Auxerre. Accordingly, William heads the names of the commission.

Next comes Simon of Authie. He is Canon of Amiens, with a chair also in the University.[1] A notice of him, recently discovered, speaks of him as a very learned man.[2] The Pontiff, on account of his impartial spirit, appoints him with others to inquire into the disturbance between Town and Gown, in the quarter of St. Marcellas, in which several students were killed.[3] Again, we find him commissioned to procure the restoration of some professors to their chairs.[4] Next to the name of Simon is that of Stephen of Provins. He also in an especial degree holds the confidence and esteem of the Holy Father. He is not only learned, but evidently a man of prudence and tact; for we find the Pope, some years later, assigning to him the delicate mission of settling a long-standing and widely known dispute between a bishop and a monastery.[5] He is also to be remembered as a friend and patron of Michael

[1] Du Boulay erroneously makes him one of the Canons of Paris.

[2] Discovered at Amiens by Dom Grenier, and published by M. Paulin Paris. It reads thus: " Mense novembris, obiit magister Simon de Alteia, vir litteratissimus, hujus ecclesiæ canonicus" (*Notices et Extraits des MSS.*, tom. xxi. 2ième partie, p. 222).

[3] The letter bears date of April 19, 1231. It is to be found in Du Boulay, tom. iii. p. 144.

[4] Ibid., p. 146.

[5] The bishop was of Tournay and the monastery was of St. Pierre-du-Gand. The letter is dated December 15, 1234. See *Notices des MSS.*, loc. cit.

Scott, and sufficiently an admirer of Aristotle to enable Michael to dedicate to him one of his translations.[1]

Such are the men into whose hands Gregory places the prohibited books for examination. He empowers them, in a brief, bearing date of April 20, 1231, to examine the books with all due attention and rigour, and scrupulously to retrench every error calculated to scandalize or in the least offend the readers of them, in order that the said books, without delay and without danger, may be restored to their places in the course of study. Three days later, Gregory still further shows his good will towards the students of Aristotle: he writes to the Abbé of St. Victor's and the Prior of the Dominicans, empowering them to absolve both masters and students from all censures that they might have incurred in

---

[1] The translation is of the book *De Cœlo et Mundo*. The dedication runs as follows :—" Tibi Stephane de Pruvino, hoc opus, quod ego Michael Scotus dedi latinitati ex dictis Aristotelis, specialiter commendo" (Jourdain, *Recherches Critiques sur les Traductions d'Aristote*, p. 127).

[2] This important document was the missing link in the chain of evidence the absence of which has led to so much confusion among the historians of this period of thought. It proves that the Church brought the remedy herself, and encouraged the study of Aristotle, instead of being silently overborne by the strong current in his favour, as is generally represented. Tiraboschi thinks the prohibition was confined to the University of Paris (*Storia della Letteratura Italiana*, tom. iv. p. 174). Talamo discusses the issue, but is not aware of the existence of this document (*L'Aristotelismo della Scolastica nella Storia della Filosofia*, 1873). Emile Charles, in his able study upon Roger Bacon, also discusses the question, but does not use this document. We give the full text in an Appendix.

reading the prohibited books.¹ Nor is this all. In May 5, of the same year, His Holiness commissions Simon of Authie and the Dean of Soissons to make every effort to restore peace in the University, and order in the studies so long disturbed.² A new spirit is breathed into the University. Du Boulay writes: "In the year 1231, the Muses, after two years of banishment, begin to flourish once more in Paris, and study and discipline are being restored."³ The struggle is over. The crisis has passed. Aristotle is fully recognized. Michael Scott may now put forth his translations of the Stagyrite. And in fact, it is precisely about this time, Roger Bacon tells us, that Michael Scott appears upon the scene, bringing with him especially the treatise on Physics with the commentaries thereon; and from this time forth Aristotle is held in high esteem by the Latins.⁴ It would seem as though the venerable Pontiff, with his far-reaching wisdom, had seen through the vista of the ages the extent of Aristotle's growing influence, and had resolved to crown his long and glorious career with this act of restoring his philosophy to its proper place. Now that Aristotle is enthroned, a new impetus is given to the study of his writings.

[1] Du Boulay, tom. iii. p. 144. [2] Ibid., p. 146. [3] Ibid., p. 140.
[4] "Tempore Michael Scoti, qui annis Domini 1230 transactus apparuit, deferens librorum Aristotelis partes aliquas de naturalibus et mathematicis, cum expositoribus sapientibus, magnificata est philosophia Aristotelis apud Latinos" (*Opus Majus*, pp. 36, 37).

VIII.

ARISTOTLE IN THE UNIVERSITY.

WE know not to what extent the restored books were corrected. The strictures of the commission cannot have been very severe, since we find the most objectionable passages in the condemned books paraphrased by Albertus Magnus (1193–1280). "Our censors," says Hauréau, "would undoubtedly have marked these passages, but without cutting them out; later on the remembrance of those prudent notes being lost, there would be found persons bold enough, not only to expound, but even to justify the whole of the Physics."[1] Roger Bacon fixes the date of 1237 as that prior to which all censure ceased to attach to the reading of the prohibited books.[2] Whatever the corrections may have been, they were soon swept away by the spirit of rationalism. No temporary torrent it, as Philip de Grève would have us regard its influx. More and more does it gain

---

[1] In *Notices et Extraits des MSS.*, tom. xxi. p. 227.
[2] Emile Charles, *Roger Bacon*, p. 412.

ground, and greater and greater is the havoc that it plays among young and old in the University. Religious studies have grown distasteful. Eudes, another Chancellor, sums up the statement of affairs at this period when he complains that the men of his day spend their whole time in the pursuit of secular knowledge and seem to care nothing for the science of God.[1] Roger Bacon bears witness to the continuous influence of Avicenna and Averroës in the schools.[2] In 1240, we find the Bishop of Paris condemning ten specific errors, all of them Arabo-Peripatetic in their nature.[3] In 1247, Eudes, now Papal Legate, publicly condemns two professors, John Brescian and Raimund; furthermore, he insists that logicians shall confine themselves to their own subjects and shall not meddle with questions of theology.[4] In the mean time, Aristotle's influence grows apace. A knowledge of his philosophy becomes indispensable. The University extends the course of studies so as to include nearly all his works then known. Thus, it inscribes upon the statute-books the following, upon which the student will be required to

[1] "Sed moderni totum tempus in sæculari scientia expendunt, parum vel nihil de scientia Dei curantes" (*apud* Launoy, *De Var. Arist. Fort*, p. 63).

[2] Emile Charles, *loc. cit.*, p. 314.

[3] They are reported by S. Bonaventura, *In II. Sent. Dist.*, xxiii. a. ii. quæst. iii. *in finem*.

[4] Talamo, *L'Aristotelismo della Scolastica nella Storia della Filosofia*, p. 231.

pass examinations:—The Dialectics, the Topics, the Ethics, the Physics, the Metaphysics and the Natural History; the book on the Heavens; that on Meteors and that on Generation; the spurious book on Causality; the books on Sensation, on Sleep and Waking, on Plants, on the Distinction of Spirit and Soul, on Memory, and on Life and Death.[1] May we not say that Aristotle has monopolized the whole course of study? That which is his, and that which is not his, but which simply bears his name, are read without discrimination. Error must needs grow out of such uncritical reading. The Church continues to exercise all due vigilance. Alexander IV. invites Albert the Great to refute the errors that are rife.[2] Again, it is found necessary to expurge

---

[1] It is interesting to note the distribution of those varied subjects. After mentioning the Dialectics, Topics, and Ethics, the statute continues: "Physicam Aristotelis, Metaphysicam et librum de Animalibus *in festo S. Joannis Baptistæ*. Librum Cœli et Mundi, librum 1. Meteororum cum 4 *in Ascensione*. Librum de Anima si cum Naturalibus legatur, *in festo Ascensionis*: si autem cum Logicalibus, *in festo Annunciationis B. Virginis*. Librum de Generatione, *in Cathedra S. Petri*. Librum de Causis, *in 7 septimanis*. Librum de Sensu et Sensato, *in 6 septimanis*. Librum de Somno et Vigilia, *in 5 septimanis*. Librum de Plantis, *in 5 septimanis*. Librum de Differentia Spiritus et Animæ, *in 2 septimanis*. Librum de Memoria et Reminiscentia, *in 2 septimanis*. Librum de Morte et Vita, *in una septimana*" (Du Boulay, *Hist. Univ. Par.*, tom. iii. pp. 280, 281).

[2] Albert tells us that he wrote his Exposition of the Gospel of St. John "ad instantiam Alexandri IV., pro extirpandis hæresibus tunc vigentibus Romæ lecta." Again, after refuting the pantheistic

the Physics and the Metaphysics. Neither master nor student seems desirous to discriminate between the doctrine that is conformable and the doctrine that is opposed to the teachings of revealed religion. Indeed, a fundamental proposition, held by many of that day was that a statement may be true in philosophy and yet contrary to Faith, or true according to Faith and false according to reason. It is an old error which the Church has had to contend with from the beginning. It is the last subterfuge of a soul believing and yet carried away by intellectual inflation. And it is in order to remove this stumbling-block from such souls that Urban IV., in a Bull to the University, forbids any further reading of the Physics and Metaphysics until they shall have been freed from all the doctrines contrary to the Faith.[1]

Here, too, has it been asserted that this prohibition of Urban was the outcome of the continuous opposition of Rome to Aristotle; here, too, have those making the charge been mistaken. The quarrel is not between Rome and Aristotle; it is between the Church and the irresponsible rationalism of the day. No greater patron

doctrine of a universal intellect actuating all minds, he says: "Hæc omnia aliquando collegi in curia existens ad præceptum Domini Alexandri Papæ, et factus fuit inde libellus quem multi habent et intitulatur *Contra Errores Averroës* et hic etiam posita sunt ut perfectior scientia Summæ" (*Sum. Theol.*, part. ii. tr. xiii. q. 77, m. 3, *Opp.*, tom. xviii.).

[1] Du Boulay, *Hist. Univ. Par.*, tom. iii. p. 365.

of learning was there than Pope Urban IV. And in an especial manner was he a patron of philosophy. "To Urban IV.," says Tiraboschi, "is due, by all right and title, the glory of having revived philosophy in Italy."[1] One year previous to the issuing of this Bull, in 1261, Urban called to Rome the Angelical Doctor, and had him to comment upon the very works, the reading of which for the time being he was prohibiting in Paris. " About this time," says the historian, " Brother Thomas did and wrote much at the request of Urban. . . . Professing in Rome, he gathered together nearly the whole of philosophy, both natural and moral, and wrote commentaries thereon; but chiefly upon the Ethics and the Metaphysics, which he treated in a novel and peculiar manner."[2] Urban appreciates Aristotle, but he prizes still more the souls of the youths of Paris who are led astray from the teachings of the Church by false doctrines imposed upon them in the name of Aristotle. For him to act otherwise would be a betrayal of his trust

[1] *Storia della Letteratura Italiana*, tom. iv. p. 170. Tiraboschi here prints the dedication of a mathematical work to Urban, by Campano de Navarre, in which Urban is eulogized as the patron and protector of philosophy.

[2] " Tunc frater Thomas redit de Parisiis ex certis caussis, et ad petitionem Urbani multa fecit et scripsit. . . . Isto autem tempore Thomas tenens studium Romæ, quasi totam philosophiam sive moralem sive naturalem exposuit, et in scriptum, seu commentem redegit: sed præcipue Ethicam et Metaphysicam, quodam singulari et novo modo tradendi (Tolomæus, *Hist. Eccles.*, lib. xxii. cap. xxiv. p. 1154. In vol. xi., *Rerum Italicarum Scriptores*).

as guardian of the faith and morals of Christendom. Hence his action in reviving the prohibition of Gregory.

But for all that, the spirit of rationalism is not checked. Indeed, every effort made to check it, seems to cause it to become more rampant. Stephen Tempier, the Bishop of Paris, in 1268, sounds the alarm. He assembles the Church and University authorities. They discuss and condemn some of the leading errors afloat. Among them are many long known to the student of philosophy: that the intellect of all men is numerically one and identical; that the world is eternal; that the human will wishes and chooses by necessity. The assembly admonishes the Rectors and Proctors of the diverse faculties that things pertaining to Faith be not discussed in schools of philosophy, lest weak minds, in attempting to grasp its inscrutable mysteries should be led to disbelieve or doubt them altogether.[1] And not alone obscure and reckless men held and taught the condemned propositions; they were publicly broached and discussed by masters of the highest reputation.[2] The ablest men in the Church are called upon to cope with them, and to protect the teachings of Christian philosophy against the encroachment of rationalism. Brother Gilles of the Dominican Order begs Albert the Great to write a

[1] Du Boulay, *Hist. Univ. Par.*, tom. iii. p. 397.
[2] "Articulos quos in scholis proponunt Magistri Parisiis, qui in Philosophia majores reputantur" (Letter of Egidius to Albert the Great. See Sighart, *Vie de Albert le Grand*, cap. xxv. p. 272).

refutation of the condemned propositions. Albert, though arrived at that period in life when men who have borne the heat and the burden of the day seek repose, took his pen and wrote a vigorous tract against them.[1] Aquinas is recalled to Paris to resume his lessons. He also writes an unsparing refutation of the errors afloat.[2] The University makes it matter of expulsion for any professor of philosophy to broach in public any theological question, if within a given time after receiving warning he recall not what he has said. Also, if in public disputations, he should decide any question against what is of Faith, he shall be expelled unless he makes public retraction and reparation.[3] The struggle grows more intense. The University forbids public discussion of Averroistic doctrines; they become a general topic of private discussion and private tuition. Banished from the chairs, they are whispered in corners and in closets. St. Thomas alludes to this subterfuge in his tract against them: "All that we have written against this error," says he—he is alluding to the error of the unity of the human intellect—"is not from the evidences of Faith, but from the sayings and reasonings of philosophers themselves. Still, should some author, inflated with pride through false science, desire to refute what we

---

[1] *Opusculum. Opp.*, tom. xxi.
[2] Tract, *Contra Averroistas.*
[3] Statute, April 1, 1271, *apud* Du Boulay, tom. iii. p. 398.

have advanced, let him not speak in corners, nor before boys incapable of pronouncing upon such arduous questions; but if he dares, let him refute our writing. He will then find, not only in me who am least of all, but in many others as well, those who are sustainers of the truth, and by whom his errors will be refuted and his ignorance reclaimed."[1] The University, in consequence, raises its voice against the teaching of theology and philosophy in private, and everywhere outside of the regularly appointed chairs.[2]

Through all this strife with rationalism, perhaps all the better because of the strife, have the Schoolmen, to all intents and purposes, completed their work. Thomas is dead, and Bonaventura is dead, and Albert is fast approaching the close of his long and wonderful career. But the rationalistic influx grows broader and deeper. The condemned errors are no longer counted by the tens; they are counted by the hundreds.[3] They extend to Oxford, and it is found needful that the same syllabus of them be there introduced.[4] All Europe seems flooded with the doctrines that flow from the Eternal Gospel,

[1] *Opusculum*, xv. *De Unitate Intellectus Contra Averroistas, in finem*. *Opp.*, tom. xvi. p. 224.

[2] Statute of 1276, *Stat. Universit. Contra docentes Theolog. in locis privatis*, Du Boulay, tom. iii. p. 430.

[3] See the Syllabus of errors afloat in the Paris University, prepared in 1277, at the request of Pope John XXI. (Du Boulay, ibid., pp. 434-444).

[4] In 1284, by Robert Kilwardby, Archbishop of Canterbury.

from Amaury, from David of Dinant, from Averroës. These are the tares of the teeming intellectual activity that the thirteenth century produced. Women become infected with the new doctrines and believe themselves heaven sent. The Beguin Wilhelmina, of Milan, represents herself as the Holy Ghost, and miracles are said to have been worked at her tomb.[1] An Englishwoman, beautiful and eloquent, passes through Italy, teaching that the Holy Ghost has become incarnate in her for the redemption of woman.[2] These are only a few of the many wild vagaries that thrived, directly or indirectly, under the shadow of Arabo-Aristotelian teachings.

Lastly, now that in the vast storehouses of an Albert and a Thomas—not to mention an Alexander of Hales, a Bonaventura, and others only a little less renowned— are to be found the method and the principles of refutation of all possible objections that can be raised in the name of Aristotle; now that it has been proved that if adversaries of the Faith find in him weapons of attack, its defenders find also in him no less effective weapons of resistance, the Church pays his genius a crowning honour. She herself installs him in the University. In 1366, two Cardinal Legates from Pope Urban V., deputed to reform the University in all its faculties, make obligatory upon all aspiring to the Bachelor's Degree the

---

[1] Muratori, *Antiq. Ital. Med. Ævi*, tom. v. col. 90–93.
[2] *Vide* Le Clerc, *Hist. Litt. de la France*, tom. xxiv. p. 117.

study of the Logic and Psychology of Aristotle. Nor can any one receive his Master's Degree, who has not read the Physics, the Metaphysics, the Ethics and the minor works of the Stagyrite.[1] "Henceforth," says Hauréau, after noticing this event, "Aristotle shall be the universal teacher."[2] Yes, in a certain sense. We shall determine that sense by inquiring into the spirit in which the great minds among the Schoolmen accepted Aristotle as Master. Were they mere formalists repeating or imitating the Philosopher? The accusation has been made and the impression remains. With what justice we shall see.

[1] We here give that part of the statute bearing upon Aristotle: "Item quod audiverint veterem artem totam, librum Topicorum, quoad 4 libros et libros Elenchorum, priorum aut posteriorum complete, etiam librum de Anima in toto vel in parte. . . .

"Item quod nullus admittatur ad Licentiam in dicta Facultate, nec in examine B. Mariæ, nec in examine B. Genovesæ, nisi ulterius predictos libros audiverit Parisius, vel in alio studio generali librum Physicorum, de Generatione et Corruptione, de Cœlo et Mundo, Parva Naturalia, videlicet libros de Sensu et Sensato, de Somno et Vigilia, de Memoria et Reminiscentia, de longitudine et brevitate vitæ, librum Mechanicæ, vel qui actu audiat eundem, et quod aliquos libros Mathematicos audiverit.

"Item quod nullus de cætero admittatur ad Magisterium in Artibus, nisi prædictos libros audiverit, nec non libros morales, specialiter librum Ethicorum pro majori parte et librum Metheororum, saltem tres primos libros omni dispensatione interdictâ" (Bulæus, *Hist. Univ. Par.*, tom. iv. p. 390).

[2] *Hist. de la Phil. Schol.*, tom. ii. cap. vi. p. 108.

IX.

LIMITATIONS OF THOUGHT.

It is noteworthy that the great thinkers of this golden era of mediæval thought were also saintly characters, and docile children of the Church. They appreciated the Faith that was in them, and knowing it to be a free and sovereign gift beyond their power of meriting, they sought to preserve and defend it by prayerful study. They ever kept in mind that the truths of Divine revelation are to be accepted on their own grounds; nor did they forget that the truths of reason, though coming home to them in another manner and upon different grounds, cannot in any sense contradict those of revelation; for they recognized that both revealed truth and natural truth are of God. They believed in the Supernatural Order. They held to a world of grace, above and beyond the world of Nature; each distinct in its kind; each a living reality. They regarded the Church as the visible medium through which these two worlds met and merged. She was to them the sacred repository of those Divine truths that human reason, by its own unaided lights, was unable to grasp; upon her authority alone did they accept them as certain. They held with St. Paul, that no man can think a good thought as of himself without the assistance of Him in Whom we live, move, and are.[1] No more can he think the true, except as it is given him to think it, according to the primary conditions implanted in his rational nature, and in obedience to the laws of the human intellect. This has been clearly expressed by the great light and glory of the Schoolmen. "God helps man," says St. Thomas, "to understand that which He Himself directly proposes, not only by means of the object, or by increase of light; but the natural light that makes of man an intelligent being comes also from God; and furthermore, God being the Primary Truth from Whom all other truths derive their certitude—even as in the demonstrative sciences, secondary propositions derive their certitude from the primary ones—nothing could be certain in the intellect, save by Divine Power, just as in the sciences no conclusions are certain except by virtue of first principles."[2]

Accordingly, the Schoolmen drew clear lines between matters of faith and matters of reason. As clerics and monks, they studied philosophy, rarely for its own sake,

---

[1] 2 Cor. iii. 4.
[2] *Compend. Theol. ad Fr. Reginaldum*, cap. cxxix. *Opp.*, tom. xvi. p. 34.

frequently with view of developing, explaining, or defending the Christian truths, always in a spirit of docility to the Church. Nor were they, in accepting these religious limitations, labouring under any disadvantage. Religion has answered many a pressing question long before reason had time to reach its solution. Was the rational solution any the less valid because the result to be reached was already known? Take those who broke down all barriers between the two orders. Have they derived therefrom any real benefit? There are the Neo-Platonists. They placed no bounds to their speculations; they indulged in the wildest vagaries, and called them systems; they sank all religious truth into their oriental imaginings; they were the all-knowing and the all-wise. Now, what real addition — as the legitimate outcome of all their theorizings—have they made to the sum of thought? What Neo-Platonic truth does the world accept to-day as of primary importance in life or in philosophy? Or take the Averroists. We have seen the havoc which they played amongst the Schoolmen. Leagued and sworn as they had been in every University, to propagate their doctrines; seriously as they threatened to overwhelm Christian science, to what purpose has it all been? In vain do we look for any clearly defined truth, or body of truths, that we can accept as an addition to mental or metaphysical science. All is lost in the arid sand of speculation. Can the same be said of their opponents? Who dares say—knowing whereof he speaks—that human thought is not the richer for the labours of an Aquinas and a Roger Bacon? And yet their faith was simple, their piety sincere, their loyalty and devotion to mother Church unswerving. Think you their religious belief hampered their scientific thought? To think so were to ignore the workings of the human mind and the primary laws of thought.

Thought must be free; thought is necessarily free. But it does not follow that thought has not its limitations. It has; it is restricted on many sides; and without restriction there is no continuous train of thought, and therefore no reasoning. A glance at the limitations of thought will enable us to understand its nature and its workings. To begin with, there are the essential limitations of reason, within which reason follows out certain laws and acts under certain conditions. The mind, as thinking-subject, must take itself for granted. Turn whither it will, the I-am-I of its own identity faces it as a fact, outside of which it cannot move. It must accept upon trust the acts of its memory. There is no thinking without receiving as truthfully reported that which the memory records. It must accept the primary principle of all demonstration. "It is evident," says Aristotle, "that it is impossible for the same inquirer to suppose that at the same time the same thing should be and should not be."[1] Even the reason of an Aristotle, searching and acute though it be, cannot work without that principle, nor can it by any possible ingenuity transgress its limitation. In like manner, is it equally impossible for the human intellect to think two and two to be three, or five, or aught else than four. It may, in reasoning upon erroneous or ill-understood premises, deduce a consequence that were equivalent to the proposition that two and two make three or make five; we all of us do it in a measure when we overleap or fall short of the truth. But the moment the intellect perceives its error, however slow it may be to express that it was in the wrong, it rebounds at once to its normal condition and thinks the eternal truth that two and two make four. For the intellect can only think the true as true.[2] Nor are those primary conditions and accompaniments of thinking its only limitations.

Thought has also its restrictions from without. There is the restraint of mental discipline, in which the will compels the intellect to exclude all matters extraneous to that upon which it is then and there occupied, and to

---

[1] *Metaphysics*, III., iii. 9.

[2] "Objectum autem proprium intellectus est quidditas rei. Unde circa quidditatem rei, per se loquendo, intellectus non fallitur; sed circa ea quæ circumstant rei essentiam vel quidditatem intellectus potest falli, dum unum ordinat ad aliud, vel componendo, vel dividendo, vel etiam ratiocinando" (*Summa Theol.*, I. i. quæst. lxxxv. art. vi. c.).

move in a given direction. Without this strain there is no real thinking; without it, it were impossible to prolong a train of thought to its legitimate conclusion, or properly to exhaust the consideration of a proposition. There is the restriction of language. Our thought takes colour and shape from the speech in which it is expressed. Our very idioms mould its form. Take any subject; submit its treatment to a French and a German mind; you will find the genius of each language materially affecting the respective thoughts of each intellect.[1] Then there is the restriction of the schools. Each school has its own mould of expression. The disciple thinks in the terms of his school. In all his reasoning he is on his guard against admitting any form of expression that might be construed into an admission of the views of another school. This is a great hardship, frequently a great tyranny, for the human intellect. It drags it into partisanship. The disciple of Schopenhauer feels in duty bound to tear Hegel to tatters. The Agnostic is not happy unless he is abusing religion as the enemy of material progress. To belong exclusively to any one school of thought is to shut out from one's soul all truth but that which presents itself under a given aspect. It is to be continually asking the question,

---

[1] As an illustration, compare the modes in which Descartes and Fichte both establish the fact of their personal identity as an assumption beyond which they cannot pass.

Can any good come out of Nazareth? And yet good can come out of Nazareth; every Nazareth of thought has its own lesson to teach us if we willingly learn it and put it to profit. Finally, there is the intellectual atmosphere of the day, in which thought lives and moves. It cannot exist without breathing this air. If the past is revived, it lives only in proportion as it is brought to bear upon the present. Unconsciously do we breathe this atmosphere. It enters into our language; it moulds our phrases; it colours our thinking. It is a subtle essence ever present yet ever eluding our grasp.

Now, the atmosphere of the golden era of the Middle Ages, is the Spirit of Faith. It speaks in the Crusades. It breathes in the Gothic cathedral. It is the inspiration alike of Dante and Aquinas. All the great intellects of that epoch breathed this atmosphere of Faith. It gave life and colour to their thoughts. It raised them above themselves into the supernatural life which they touched and felt as a living reality. Scepticism was foreign to the minds of an Albert, a Bonaventura, a Thomas, and a Roger Bacon. Therefore, in all their studies and speculations they were as little disturbed and under no greater restraint than was Plato or Aristotle. To one whose doubts are his life—whose sole object is the pursuit of truth whilst sceptical of its existence—this frame of mind is indeed an enigma; but it is no less a fact. No religious believer finds embarrassment in holding by truths of Faith and at the same time carrying out a course of reasoning as freely as the most confirmed sceptic. His conclusion may be found to clash with some article of his Faith. Be it so. The revealed truth has possession. That admits of no revision. Not so the conclusion. Experience has taught the reasoner how likely he is to go astray in pursuing a line of argument; how frequently some misplaced or some ill-understood term has stolen into his premises and vitiated the whole of his reasoning; or how some fact has been overlooked, in consequence of which he finds his conclusion at variance with existing facts. In all such instances, his only remedy is to revise his chain of reasoning and rid himself of the cause of the fallacy running through it. Therefore, should he perceive any such discrepancy, it remains for him to go over his whole argument once more; and should he still find no error, or if he is yet unable to bring his conclusion into harmony with the revealed truth, he is not thereby disturbed. He awaits additional light flowing from a larger experience and more advanced science. The overhasty conclusion has damaged science; the overhasty censure has brought odium upon religion. To him who has learned how to labour and how to wait the light comes. This is the lesson of the history of thought. Never yet has a revealed truth stood in the way of a scientific truth rightly demonstrated. On the contrary, he who is possessed of the great truths of revealed religion, and holds them with a grasp of living conviction, has always a norm with which to compare and adjust any other truths coming within the domain of those that are of revelation. He is saved time and trouble; he treads the mazes of thought with a firm step; he brings his investigations into other spheres of study with a calm spirit. Here is to be found the inspiring principle of the great intellects of mediæval days.

X.

THE SPIRIT IN WHICH THE SCHOOLMEN WORKED.

IN full freedom of spirit, then, did the Schoolmen labour. They commented Aristotle; they put forth philosophical speculations; they developed theological science; they observed and studied the laws of Nature, making serious though ineffectual efforts to rend the veil and wrench her secrets from her keeping, without suffering the least embarrassment from the Faith that was their life. We have seen the Church set down as a primary rule of action, that the theologian should not attempt to rationalize the mysteries of religion,[1] and that, in the stead, he should cultivate the Early Fathers and the Sacred Scriptures; also that the philosophers should not trespass upon the preserves of theology. "There is not," says an impartial witness who has made a thorough study of the Schoolmen, and who has learned to appreciate them, "there is not a logician of the thir-

[1] The letter of Gregory IX. in 1228, already referred to, is especially strong on this point: "non profectum aliquem auditorum, ut sic videantur non theodacti, seu theologi, sed potius theophanti" (Raynaud, *Ad. Annal. Baron.*, tom. i. p. 615).

teenth century, who, on assuming his seat, does not begin with the declaration that, this chair not being one of theology, he will place beyond all controversy the mysteries and sacraments in order solely to discuss those questions not interdicted by authority. It is not recent doctors, then, who drew the line of distinction between the two domains; the Middle Ages recognized it, professed it, and more or less scrupulously acted upon it."[1] Let us for a moment look into the works of a few of the great Schoolmen and note the spirit that guided their pen.

There is Albert the Great (1193-1280). The vastness of his labours is appalling. The wide range of subjects which his genius took in by way of summaries, commentaries, and tracts—philosophy, theology, mathematics, natural history in its chief branches, physics, astronomy, mechanical engineering; sermons and lectures upon spiritual subjects; the very list of them would fill a volume[2]—and upon which he gave out thoughts original and striking, has well merited for him the title of Universal Doctor. How did this untiring genius enter upon his studies? Here are his words: "A philosopher should admit nothing without sufficient reason, for it

[1] Hauréau, *Hist. de la Phil. Schol.*, tom. i. p. 31; Thurot, *De l'Organisation de l'Enseignement dans l'Université de Paris au Moyen Age*. Paris, 1850, pp. 124 *sqq*.

[2] For a list of Albert's writings see his biography by Sighart, pp. 452-476, French edition.

is a desire innate to all of us to know the causes of things natural, to study their properties and to seize their differences."[1] Have they not the ring of an extract from some modern scientist? Again, in the same spirit he advises his brethren to study Nature, not for the sake of explaining her prodigies, but for the better understanding of her ordinary laws: "We are not to seek in Nature how God, according to His good pleasure, employs creatures to work the prodigies by which He makes His power so striking, but rather such phenomena as are of ordinary occurrence and act according to natural causes."[2] Here is the spirit of modern scientific investigation. This man, so just in his remarks, so correct in his method of approaching philosophical subjects, has been accused of the basest subserviency to Aristotle. Undoubtedly the Master has great weight with him; but he knows how to discriminate between the truth and error in his writings. "Whoever believes Aristotle to be God," he tells us, "may also believe him never to be in the wrong; but admitting him to be a man, then unquestionably may he err like the rest of us."[3] And elsewhere he states the principle

[1] " Philosophi proprium est non dicere aliquid nisi cum ratione et causa: cupiditas enim nostra est inquisitio causæ omnium rerum naturalium, et consideratio proprietatum et differentiarum earum: quia talia in physica convenit nos dicere docendo, et convenit aliis talia a nobis audire" (Lib. ii. *Meteororum*, tract. ii. cap. i. p. 43).

[2] Lib. i. *De Cælo & Mundo*, tract. iv. cap. x. p. 75.

[3] " Qui credit Aristotelem fuisse Deum, ille debet credere quod

of this philosophical independence: "It may behove the Pythagoreans to swear by the word of the Master; for our part, we are content to receive the word when its truth shall have been proven by reason."[1] Because he sought to make Aristotle his own in this independent spirit, did he merit to have it said of him: "Never was the doctrine of Aristotle treated with greater scope and even depth."[2] We are not surprised that the timid chronicler should represent Albert as a man drunk with the wine of profane wisdom.[3] But, it may be asked, how far in actual practice did Albert verify all these fine words of his? We will take him in natural science, and we will bring a competent witness to testify. But we must not forget that the age was one of many scientific superstitions, when astrology was identified with astronomy, and alchemy with chemistry,[4] and fantastic explanations took the place of experimental investigation, then

nunquam erravit. Si autem credit ipsum esse hominem, tunc procul dubio errare potuit sicut et nos" (Lib. viii. *Physicorum*, tract. i. cap. xiv. *Opp.*, tom. ii. p. 332).

[1] *Opera*, tom. i. p. 238, edit. 1651. Sighart says: "He declares in a hundred places: 'Here Aristotle was wrong'" (*Vie d'Albert le Grand*, p. 482).

[2] J. Barthélemy St. Hilaire, *La Logique d'Aristote*, tom. ii. p. 225.

[3] Langius Monachus Cizensis, in *Chron. Ad An.*, 1258. See Emile Charles, *Roger Bacon*, p. 144.

[4] Still from Albert have we received that useful term *affinity* in modern chemistry. See Pouchet, *Histoire des Sciences Naturelles au Moyen Age*, p. 310.

unthought of. From it all Albert was not free. None the less do gleams of light run across his pages. They excite the warm admiration of Humboldt. He is surprised at the delicacy of observation betrayed in Albert's reasonings upon the structure and physiology of plants;[1] upon the simultaneous dependence of climate on latitude and elevation, and the effect of different angles of the sun's rays in heating the earth; upon the influence of mountains in determining the warmth or coldness of a locality.[2] They seem to him far and away beyond the epoch in which lived "this man of vast erudition."[3]

But the chief fruit and glory of the life and labours of Albert, was Thomas Aquinas (1227–1274). It is the great merit of the Angelical Doctor that he knew how to blend with admirable tact the doctrines of the Church and the teachings of human reason. He holds that philosophy is good and useful and in a measure necessary for the discussion of those natural truths that are the preambles of Faith, amongst which he includes the existence of God;[4] no less good and necessary is it as a means of refuting difficulties raised against the

[1] *Cosmos*, vol. ii. p. 618, tr. E. C. Otté. Bohn's Library.
[2] *Examen Critique de l'Histoire de la Géographie du Nouveau Continent*, tom. i. p. 55 note.
[3] Ibid. Humboldt calls his *Liber Cosmographicus de Natura Locorum* a species of Physical Geography.
[4] *Summa Theol.*, I. i. quæst. ii. art. ii. ad. 1.

dogmas of religion. The higher truths and mysteries transcending the reach of human reason, in the spirit of a true philosopher, he accepts upon authority.[1] He is unwearied in laying stress upon the fundamental principle that between the truths of reason and the truths of revelation, when rightly understood, there is neither divergence nor discord.[2] "Since grace," he tells us, in his masterpiece, "does not destroy nature, but rather betters it, therefore should natural reason minister unto faith just as the natural bent of the will should aid charity."[3]

And in another place he puts the question directly as to whether theological questions should be answered upon the principle of authority or upon that of reason; and his reply is, that, if repelling the doubts of an adversary, the adversary should be met upon his own grounds and his own arguments made use of. "Such arguments," he adds, "should be employed as show the why and wherefore of the thing, otherwise we would know that a thing is so, but would acquire no knowledge concerning it."[4] And how aptly St. Thomas could bring to bear the scientific spirit upon scientific work, is well illustrated in his comment upon the various explanations made by Aristotle and others to account for the diverse movements of the

---

[1] *Summa Contra Gentiles*, lib. i. cap. ix. p. 6.
[2] Super Bëotium, *De Trinitate Opusc.*, lxx. quæst. ii. a, iii. c.
[3] *Summa Theol.*, I. i. quæst. i. art. viii. ad. 2.
[4] *Quodlibetum*, IV. art. xviii. c. p. 517.

planets. He is not satisfied with any of them. These suppositions need not be taken as the true solution; they only seem to explain the facts; by some other way not yet known of men may their motion be explained.[1] Could Charles Darwin, who was a model of scientific modesty, be more guarded?

Finally, note the spirit in which Roger Bacon (1214-1294) laboured. Born out of his due time centuries too early, he finds himself out of place in his age. He loathes Scholasticism as heartily as Descartes. He abuses nearly all of his contemporaries. He abuses Albert; he abuses Thomas; he abuses Bonaventura; he abuses Michael Scott; he loads abuse upon Alexander of Hales. He has no sympathy for "those tractates and summæ—horse-loads composed by many—and not at all with the most holy text of God."[2] He has the soul of a humanist in his love for philology. He looks upon a thorough study of the languages as the basis of all true scholarship and sound criticism. He has the soul of the

---

[1] This remarkable passage is so truly in the spirit of modern scientific thought that we give the full text: "Illorum autem suppositiones quas adiovenerunt, non est necessarium esse veras: licet enim talibus suppositionibus factis appareant solvere, non tamen oportet dicere has suppositiones esse veras: quia forte secundum aliquem alium modum nondum ab hominibus comprehensum, apparentia circa stellas salvantur. Aristoteles tamen utitur hujusmodi suppositionibus ad qualitatem motuum tamquam veris" (In lib. ii. *De Cælo*, lect. xvii. p. 120).

[2] *Opera Minora*, preface, p. lvii. Rolls Series. London, 1859.

Baron of Verulam in his eager desire to promote the study of the physical sciences by means of the inductive method. His pages palpitate with disgust for what was best in his age, and with an insatiable yearning to achieve the scientific conquests of later days. That one thought takes hold of him and absorbs his attention and energy; like all men possessed of an engrossing idea, he can see good nowhere outside of the thought of his heart. He is a child of his own age only in the simplicity and earnestness of his faith and in his burning zeal for religion and morality. He too, as well as Albert and Thomas, knows how to distinguish between authority and reason, and is no less scientific in his method of inquiry. "In every science," he tells us, "the best method must be employed. . . . This method consists in placing first in order that which should be first known, the more easy before the more difficult, the general before the particular, the lesser before the greater; one should always study the things that are most useful, for life is short. And science should be so treated as to bring conviction without doubt and clearness without obscurity. But this is impossible without experiment. For we have three modes of knowing; namely, authority, reason, and experiment. Still, authority does not bring with it knowledge unless it is weighed, nor does it of itself give intelligence, but only credulity; for we believe on authority, but we do not receive from authority our understanding of the subject. Nor can reason distinguish between sophism and demonstration, unless we know the conclusion from experience and practice, as I shall prove further on in the experimental sciences. But very few have made use of this method in study, as shall appear below; and therefore secret and most important wisdom has remained hitherto unknown to the majority of learned men."[1] Remember that this passage was penned in the thirteenth century, when men were supposed to do no thinking and merely to swear by Aristotle. Whilst Bacon appreciated Aristotle, and made a careful study of him, he held in slight esteem the translations of translations, or rather the parodies of his writings then so much in vogue. And it is while declaiming against these that he bursts out into an oft-quoted but ill-understood expression: "For my part," he says, "if it were given me to dispose of the books of Aristotle, I would have them all burned; for the study of them only causes loss of time, engenders error, and propagates ignorance beyond anything imaginable."[2]

Thus do we find the three greatest and most representative intellects of the age not only thinking in the spirit of real philosophers, but in their writings we actually happen upon the roots of that immense tree of experimental science which so overshadows our own day. "It is," says Pouchet, "two men of the thirteenth

---

[1] *Opera Minora: Compendium Studii*, cap. i. p. 397.
[2] See Emile Charles, *Roger Bacon*, pp. 103, 104.

century, Albert the Great and Roger Bacon, who conceive it in all its power and fecundity, and to them must we restore the glory of having first indicated it."[1] And if documents speak truly, Aquinas himself was no less practical than the great Franciscan or his own great teacher; for among other books, which, upon the death of Thomas, the University of Paris begs from the Dominican Order, and which he had promised to send them when completed, besides an exposition of the Timæus of Plato there was a treatise upon the construction of aquaducts and machinery for raising and conducting water.[2]

But in good truth these great Schoolmen had a mission far other than that of commenting or imitating Aristotle. If they used the Stagyrite, they also used Plato; and if they used both, it was in accordance with the principle of true philosophy, which Aristotle himself sums up in these words: "We shall at first do well to look into the

[1] *Histoire des Sciences Naturelles*, p. 204; cf. Humboldt, *Cosmos*, vol. ii. pp. 396, 397.

[2] "Cæterum sperantes, quod obtemperetis Nobis cum effectu, in hac petitione devota humiliter supplicamus, ut cum quædam scripta ad Philosophiam pertinentia et spectantia Parisius inchoata ab eo, in suo recessu reliquerit imperfecta, et ipsum credamus, ubi translatus fuerat, complevisse, Nobis benevolentiâ vestrâ cito communicari procuretis, et specialiter super Librum Simplicii, super Libros de Cœlo et Mundo, et expositionem Timæi Platonis. *Ac de Aquarumconductibus et Ingeniis erigendis:* de quibus Nobis mittendis speciali promissione fecerat mentionem" (Du Boulay, *Hist. Univ. Par.*, tom. iii. p. 408).

speculations of others before us, so that if they speak not truly we may not share in the blame attached to them; and if there should be any doctrine common to them and ourselves, we will not stand alone under criticism. It is always pleasant to speak of things in a manner better, or at least not any worse, than others."[1] Children of their age, they accommodated themselves to the cravings and aspirations of their age. They therefore gave themselves to the studies that best satisfied those cravings and aspirations. Even for Roger Bacon—vehement though he be in denouncing the theological writings of his day—theological studies have a special fascination. The Arab and the Jew brought Aristotle to the door of the Schoolmen, placed him in their hands, and attempted in his name, with weapons forged in his workshop, to overthrow the doctrines and dogmas of the Church. The Schoolmen also forged weapons in the same workshop, and with them made a scientific defence of the Church, and struggled against the inroads of Arab and Jew for centuries, and routed them as completely from the intellectual field as did Castillian phalanx from the Spanish soil. And when the genius of painting represents St. Thomas in a halo of light emanating from the Godhead and reflected from the writings of Moses, the Evangelists and St. Paul on the one hand, and on the other from those of Plato and Aristotle, Averroës beneath

[1] *Metaphysics*, XIII. i. 1.

him in agony of confusion, his great Commentary overturned and transfixed to earth by a ray from the saint's writings, it but concentrates and epitomizes the contest between the intellectual forces of Christendom and rationalistic Mohammedanism.[1] But neither St. Thomas nor his co-labourers, trained as were their intellects, keen as was their philosophical insight, were mere adepts in speculation. They were earnest men, and theirs was an earnest work. It was a work of explanation and reconciliation of the truths of religion with those of reason; it was a defence both of reason and religion against the rationalism of the day. Theirs is the philosophy of theology. It is the philosophy on which the Church has built her definitions; it is the language in which she explains her dogmas and her doctrines. One who was not of the Church, but who was possessed of the truest and best instincts of the historian, has put the whole question in a nutshell: "It is absurd," says the late Professor Brewer, "to condemn the Schoolmen for their great devotion to Aristotle,[2] as if they had created his authority and not found it established; *equally absurd is it to condemn them for dialectical subtleties, when dialectical subtleties were overmatching Christianity.*

[1] Picture in the Church of St. Catherine's at Pisa, executed about 1340 by Francesco Traini. Orcagna, about 1335, under the inspiration of Dante, gives a marked place to Averroës in his great masterpiece in the Campo Santo of the same city.

[2] We have seen how that devotion was anything but slavish.

They were the men to show how Christianity was the answer to men's doubts; how Aristotle was to be reconciled with Revelation, not Revelation with Aristotle."[1]

Thus was theirs a work not only of defence, but of reconstruction as well. The Early Fathers, in their writings, and especially in the decrees of the Councils of the Church, contributed to the clear definition and explanation of many of the dogmas of Christianity. But the Greek Schism on the one hand, and the incursions of the barbarian on the other, checked the progress of their work. The Schoolmen took up the scattered shreds and wove them into a complete science of religion. If they used Aristotle, they were only walking in the footsteps and following the counsel of the great teachers who had gone before them. "If," says St. Augustine, "we find that those who are called philosophers should happen to say some things that are true and that can be adapted to our faith, we are justified in using them."[2] The Schoolmen took indeed the literal form of Aristotle, but they gave it a new sense. They breathed into the dry bones that passed down to them among the wrecks of other civilizations, and forthwith the dry bones became a thing of life. Another spirit

---

[1] *Monumenta Franciscana*, Rolls Series, vol. i. Preface, p. iii.

[2] "Philosophi autem qui vocantur, si qua forte vera et fidei nostræ accommodata dixerunt ⸺ . . . non solum formidanda non sunt, sed ab eis etiam tanquam injustis possessoribus in usum nostrum vindicanda" (*De Doctrin. Christian.*, l. ii. cap. 40).

animates them. The philosophy of the Schoolmen is as different from the philosophy of Aristotle, as the nature of the sturdy oak is from that of the soil in which it is rooted. A cursory comparison of both will reveal to us the intrinsic difference.

XI.

ARISTOTLE AND THE SCHOOLMEN IN METAPHYSICS AND PSYCHOLOGY.

IN this comparative study we will confine ourselves chiefly to the writings of him who is the recognized exponent of the Schoolmen. The Church, through her Pontiffs, has, in no uncertain notes, proclaimed St. Thomas as her most zealous and enlightened champion. Leo XIII. caps the climax of eulogy upon him when he says: "Rightly and deservedly is he reckoned a singular safeguard and glory of the Catholic Church. . . . Greatly enriched as he was with the science of God and the science of man, he is likened to the sun; for he warmed the whole earth with the fire of his holiness, and filled the whole earth with the splendour of his teaching."[1] His pages even now throb with the glow of life, and the din of battle rings through his sentences. Some of the issues that he fought are things of the past and have for us no other interest than that belonging to every relic

[1] Encyclical, *Eterni Patris*, 1879.

preserved in the history of thought. For Thomas, however, they were living issues calling for a speedy solution. A large number has still for us a special interest. If we will only penetrate the dry and forbidding form of the syllogism in which the questions are put—so put because the great *Summa Theologica* was intended to be a student's handbook—we shall find that many of the old errors have survived under a new name. The same objections there made and the same refutations there given still hold good. A comparative study, therefore, of the essential doctrines of the Stagyrite and the Angelical Doctor cannot be without profit.

We shall begin with Aristotle's conception of God. It is with a certain awe we read that magnificent chapter in his Metaphysics in which he demonstrates the existence of a Prime Mover and First Principle of all things. That a pagan philosopher, by the unaided light of reason, should acquire so clear a conception of the Godhead in Its unity and simplicity, is marvellous. Let us follow him for a moment: The eternal Something that imparts motion without being moved must be both Substance and Energy. This Immovable First Mover must be Entity; It must subsist after an excellent manner; It must be Necessary Being, and inasmuch as necessary, It must constitute the Good; It must therefore be the First Principle from which have depended Heaven and Nature. This Prime Mover must have Intelligence;

but since intelligence is activity and activity is life, It must be Eternal Life; It must be Eternal Mind. Essential energy belongs to God as His Everlasting Life. With Him life and duration are uninterrupted and eternal; and this constitutes the very essence of God.[1] It is all reasoned out with the neatest precision of his great intellect. It is one of the most golden pages in all antiquity. Well, after we shall have admired it to the full, let us enter the mind that evolved it. Nature is unveiled, and the philosopher stands face to face with the God of Nature. He has found Him as the answer to a problem. He touches him as the limit of a speculation. But God for Aristotle is not a Personal God with a loving care and interest in His creation. Elsewhere, in a chapter only less sublime than that we have been contemplating, he clearly asserts the unity and simplicity of God: "The Prime Mover is indivisible; is without parts; and has absolutely no kind of magnitude."[2] This is clear, beautiful, and true. What Aristotle fails to see is the nature and operation of God as Cause. He fails to see that the highest act of causality is creation. He fails to see how the preservative act is a continuation of the causative act. He therefore misses all the consequences of these great truths. The God of Aristotle is not a God to Whom all rational beings are responsible

[1] *Metaphysics*, XIII. vii.
[2] *Physics*, VIII. xv. § 26.

for their every thought, word, and act. "Whatever the truth concerning Him might be," says Hampden, "it was not to be expressed in the uplifting of pure hearts and hands to Him. Though the whole world might be found His temple, He was not to be worshipped as the Holiness of their shrines. Though the heavens were telling of His glory, and the stars were singing together for joy at His presence, yet no praise was to ascend to Him, the Lord of heaven and earth, in the perfumes of their altars or the poetry and music of their hymns. Thus devotion, being banished from the heart, sought a refuge for itself in the wilderness of a speculative theological philosophy."[1] The God of Aristotle is not the God of St. Thomas. The difference is marked. The God of St. Thomas is the God of Faith and Revelation, the God of the Nicene Creed, in substance One, in personality Three.

Aristotle, in grasping the conception of God's simplicity, missed that of His personality. It enters as a fundamental principle into the philosophy of St. Thomas. The Saint accepts it as the Church presents it to him. The very definition of personality he takes as he finds in a work attributed to Boëthius. There personality is defined as the individual substance of a rational nature.[2] It is not the whole of the nature; it is simply something

---

[1] *The Fathers of Greek Philosophy*, p. 48.
[2] *Summa*, I. i. quæst. xxiv. art. i.

subsisting in the nature.¹ Thus personality does not belong to the soul of man, nor does it belong to his body; but it belongs to that combination of body and soul that we call man. Neither is it something common to humanity as such; it can only be predicated of the particular man. Nor does it apply to other than rational natures. The personality of a dog or a horse has no meaning. Personality, then, is that which individualizes, completes, perfects the actuality of a rational nature. Inasmuch as God is an infinitely Intelligent Being, possessing all excellence, might reason apply to Him the conception of personality. He is most pure Actuality. His is therefore a Personal Nature.

Here, once for all, let us rid ourselves of an erroneous notion. Personality does not in any sense imply limitation. As applied to man, the conception is finite, just as the conception of any other part or attribute of man is finite. Not so, as applied to God. His Personality is only the perfect realization of His Infinite Nature. But the perfect realization of an Infinite Nature has no limitation, except Its own Infinite Actuality. In this sense alone does personality apply to God. Thus far may reason go. But Thomas does not stop here. With fear and trembling,² he enters the

---

¹ *Summa*, I. i. quæst. xxx. art. iv.
² "Ideo cum de Trinitate loquimur, cum cautela et modestia est agendum" (*Summa*, I. i. quæst. xxxi. art. ii.).

sanctuary of revelation, and contemplates the threefold personality of God as it has been made known. The Father begets the Word from all eternity; from the mutual love of the Father and the Word proceeds the Holy Ghost. We shall see him draw many practical lessons from the contemplation of this sublime mystery.

The Trinity is a subject fruitful in thought to him who would meditate upon it with reverence. The Three-in-One is all-perfect. He is self-sufficing. He is free. He may or may not create. When He does extend His activity outside of Himself He does it of His own Will. He exercises the most perfect act of causality in creating all things out of nothing. He is Infinite Goodness. He is Infinite Love. Man falls. He respects the free-will of man to such an extent that He will not prevent man from falling. He sends His Son, the Word, the Second Person of the Blessed Trinity, to assume human nature and to redeem that nature from the degradation to which Original Sin had dragged it down. He holds communion with man; He reveals to man Sacred Truths of a higher order than those man learns from Nature; He stoops to raise man up, without violating any of His laws, but simply by bringing into play—as in the case of miracles —other laws above those that ordinarily govern the conditions of time and space in which man now lives.

Note especially the great philosophic truth that is

brought out by this Christian view of God and creation. On the one hand is the Infinite First Cause; on the other, is the finite effect. Now, do what we may, we can find no expression for the relation between the finite and the infinite. State them in their mathematical bareness, and we find their relation, or their ratio, running into infinity or nothingness. How bridge over the chasm? Finiteness can never touch the infinite. Be it so. The Infinite Being is free. The Infinite Being can reach finite things. And this the Infinite Being did in the Incarnation of the Word. The Divinity touches His creation with another act beside the creative act by which He drew it from nothingness; that Divine act bridges over the chasm; God unites Himself to that being among His creatures that combines in itself both spiritual and material elements, and thus raises up His whole creation to a plane worthy of His creative and preservative power. Has it ever occurred to us what may be the infinite suggestiveness of this great truth in philosophical speculation? There is much in it for head and for heart. We have ample evidence of its life-giving force in the regenerating work of Christianity; but have we measured its power as an element in philosophy? You may say that the truth is a mystery—is of revelation—and as such has no place in philosophy. But are religious mysteries the only mysteries? Has philosophy none? Can philosophy explain the phenomena of thought, or of growth, or of organism, or of life, without landing in mystery? There are dark lines running all along the spectrum of our knowledge; for how few of them can we really account? Then, why not let in the light of revelation?

Aristotle missed the idea of creation. The Church presents it to the Christian philosopher as an article of faith. The Christian philosopher believes that in the beginning God created all things from nothing, of His own free Will, and out of His own pure Goodness. God spoke, and they were. All things are created by the Word, and according to the Divine exemplars existing in the Word. In this beautiful manner does the doctrine of the Trinity enter into the creative act. St. Thomas goes to show that it cannot be demonstrated that the world existed throughout all eternity.[1] God alone is eternal. Albert the Great grows impatient of those who ask what God was doing prior to creation. "In eternity," he says, "there is neither soon nor late, long nor short, space nor time. . . . The eternity of God is an indivisible present."[2] Neither, according to the Angelical Doctor, can we prove the creation of all things from nothingness.[3] It is a mystery if you will; but it

---

[1] *Summa*, I. i. quæst. xlvii. art. i.
[2] Lib. *Phys.*, viii. cap. i. p. 313. See also cap. vi. p. 320. *Opp.*, tom. ii. Edit. Jammy.
[3] *Summa*, ibid., art. ii.

is one willingly accepted. Indeed, it is far less a mystery than to admit that matter is not infinite and is yet eternal. At every point in which the finite touches the infinite there is a mystery; let him explain who can.[1] Thus it is that on God and His Providence, His personality, and His attributes, on creation and preservation, and the long chain of consequences that flow from these truths, do we find Christian philosophy standing upon a plane distinct from that on which the Lyceum stood.

Again, we take Aristotle's treatise on the human soul. The close argument, the clearness and simplicity of language, the terseness and homeliness of phrase and illustration—all carry us along a train of reasoning that opens up to us new avenues of thought. The union of soul and body, their unity and interdependence, are discussed and made to flow from those primary principles that run through all his philosophy. Substance may be viewed as matter; or it may be viewed as form; or it may be viewed as a combination of both matter and form.[2] While matter is in itself and by itself mere potential existence, the form gives it actuality.[3] Now, there is a principle of life in all organic bodies. But life is the process of nutrition, increase and decay going on under the activity of this principle. This principle is the soul.

---

[1] See Paul Janet, *La Crise Philosophique*, p. 164.
[2] *De Anima*, II. i. § 2.   [3] Ibid.

Soul we may therefore define as the formative principle of a body having predisposition to life.[1] The definition is admirable. The clear and rigid reasoning by which the philosopher reached it, is admirable. The Schoolmen accept it; they cannot improve upon it; they simply put it into a more condensed formula. They define the soul as the form of the body. But the soul as Aristotle conceived it, is not the soul as conceived by the Schoolmen. The soul, in the conception of the Stagyrite, is somewhat more than a vital principle, such as belongs to plant and animal; but it is also perishable and becomes annihilated when the animal organism is destroyed.[2] The soul in the conception of the Schoolmen is a spiritual substance animating a material body, imperishable, undying, immortal. Above the soul, distinct and separable from it, Divine in its origin and eternal in its nature, an everlasting existence incapable of being mingled with matter,[3] Aristotle places the creative reason, and thus, as we have seen, lays the foundation for the universal intellect of the Averroists. But the Schoolmen made no such distinction. All in the human intellect is included in the soul. And the Church endorsed their doctrine, when in the Council of Vienne, in 1311, she condemned the opinion

---

[1] *De Anima*, II. i. § 6.
[2] Ibid., I. iv. § 9.
[3] Ibid., III. v. § 2. See also I. iv. § 14; II. i. § 11. And *De Gener. Animal.*, II. iii. 10.

that the intellectual soul was not the substantial form of the body.[1]

. Recognizing with Aristotle the intimate union and interdependence of soul and body, the Schoolmen accepted the principle of Aristotle that there is nothing in the intellect which is not first in the senses.[2] But rejecting his doctrine of a creative reason distinct and separable from the soul, they sought elsewhere the explanation of that phenomenon by which the soul separates universals from particulars, and apprehends them, and reasons upon them. They went to the fountain-head. They also admitted a principle above and beyond human reason; but they recognized it to be the Divine Light, proceeding from the Word and illumining every man coming into this world.[3] From the Word proceeds that light by which our intellect thinks and reasons. "That intellectual light which is within us," says the Angel of the Schools, "is naught else than a certain participated likeness of the uncreated light in which are contained the eternal reasons."[4] And our intellect knows and apprehends truth only in the light of these eternal reasons.

---

[1] "Definientes, ut si quisquam deinceps asserere, defendere seu tenere pertinaciter presumpserit, quod anima rationalis seu intellectiva non sit forma corporis humani per se, et essentialiter, tamquam hereticus sit censendus." Labbé, *Sacrorum Conciliorum Collectio*, tom. xxv. p. 411.

[2] *De Anima*, III. iv.   [3] St. John i. 9.

[4] *Summa*, I. i. quæst. lxxxiv. art. v.

Thus is it that St. Thomas connects the active intellect [1] of the soul with the Supreme Intelligence; thus does he explain that marvellous power by which the human intellect separates the universal from the singular and makes it the object of thought.[2]

Throughout the theory of knowing developed by St. Thomas there runs a golden chain connecting all knowledge with God. He defines truth with Isaac [3] as the equation of the thing with the intellect. But this equation results from a twofold conformity: first, truth is in the intellect according as it is conformed to its principle, namely, the thing from which the intellect receives its cognition; and second, truth is in the thing according as there is conformity between itself and its principle, which is the Divine Intellect.[4] Thus does St. Thomas place all truth between the Divine Mind and the human understanding, the latter receiving its sanction and its certitude from the former. And in this elevated sphere of thought, taking in the whole scale, does he, in a sublime manner, distinguish between the different orders of intelligences according to their mode of apprehending truth. God is the Prime Intelligence, knowing all things in the light of His own Divine

---

[1] Intellectus Agens. See *Summa*, I. i. quæst. lxxix. art v.
[2] See this admirably treated in *Summa*, I. i. quæst. lxxxv., and q. lxxxvi.
[3] In lib. *De Definitionibus*. See I. i. quæst. xvi. art. ii.
[4] I. i. quæst. xvi. art. v. ad. 2.

Essence. Therein has He the plenitude of all cognitions. Now the nearer and the liker created intelligences are to God, the more they resemble Him in the mode of their knowing. And since He knows all things in the light of His Essence, which is One, the higher the scale of intelligence, the fewer is the number of ideas by means of which that intelligence knows. Thus, the superior angels have, because of their greater proximity to God, in the light of fewer ideas, a more perfect knowledge than have the inferior; and these latter have greater knowledge in a simpler conception and by means of less ideas, than have human intelligences. And so, among men, the more superior the intelligence, the greater the grasp of thought, and also the less the number of ideas.[1] Thus it is that the genius has chiefly a single idea in the light of which he resolves and explains all other ideas. Here is a doctrine with suggestiveness enough for a volume of thought. In this manner does St. Thomas construct a theory of knowing undreamed of by Aristotle. Turn we now to their relative treatment of the question of morals.

[1] *Summa*, I. i. quæst. lv. art. iii. c.

XII.

ARISTOTLE AND THE CHURCH IN MORALS.

In the department of Ethics Aristotle brings to bear the same happy method and the same keen intellectual vision that run through all his writings. He who knew how to define so well God and the human soul is only a little less happy in his analysis of the human heart; and he is so because, as we have seen, he failed to catch the intimate union between the Creator and His creatures. Still he is admirable in his treatment of virtue and vice, and of the disciplining of human character into the practice of the one and the avoidance of the other. "And," says an authority already quoted, "no greater praise can be given to a work of heathen morality than to say, as may with truth be said of the Ethical writings of Aristotle, that they contain nothing which a Christian may dispense with, no precept of life which is not an element of the Christian character;[1] and that they only

---

[1] The author's memory fails him. There are such precepts: *Ethics*, I. viii. 15, 16; also IV. iv. 5, 6.

fail in elevating the heart and the mind to objects which it needed Divine Wisdom to reveal, and a Divine Example to realize to the life."[1] That Aristotle did fall short of the Christian ideal is to be looked for. His premises could not carry him further. Holding as he did, that the soul dies with the body, he could see no other supreme aim in life, no other standard of happiness, than the highest and most perfect activity of the soul during the span of its years. And so, the outcome of his reasoning he thus expresses: "But if happiness be the exercise of virtue, it is reasonable to suppose that it is the exercise of the highest virtue; and that will be the virtue or excellence of the best part of us. Now, that part or faculty—call it reason, or what you will—which seems naturally to rule and take the lead, and to apprehend things noble and Divine—whether it be itself Divine or only the Divinest part of us—is the faculty the exercise of which, in its proper excellence, will be perfect happiness. . . . *Our conclusion, then, is that happiness is a kind of speculation or contemplation. . . . The man who exercises his reason and cultivates it, and holds it in the best condition, seems also to be the most beloved of heaven.*"[2] Herein is embodied the weak point of his system; therefrom flow others no less weak.

Again, argues the Stagyrite, since the object of virtue

---

[1] Hampden, *The Fathers of Greek Philosophy*, p. 123.
[2] *Nichomachean Ethics*, X. vii., viii.; trans. F. H. Peters.

is the attainment of the highest happiness and the chief good of this life, whatever includes these things is highest and chiefest. But, as the whole is by necessity prior to the part, the State is by nature clearly prior to the family and to the individual.[1] In the State, then, must reside the chief good for man. It is better and more complete both to attain and secure.[2] That man is good who fulfils the end and aim of the State. But the State exists, not for the sake of life only, but for the sake of a perfect and self-sufficing life.[3] The good citizen is therefore the superior of the good man. The State should mould him to its end.[4] "This," he tells us, "can only be effected if men live subject to some kind of reason and proper regimen backed by force."[5] At the last analysis, the sole sanction for the practice of virtue is that which comes from the State. The great object of living virtuously is that the State may profit thereof. The very virtues upon which the philosopher lays stress, are those most contributing to the well-being of the State. This is the meaning of individual perfection. It is not a sense of virtue that rules the community—however isolated cases may have been so influenced—so much as a sense of self-sufficiency. And this grows out of the relations of society to the State.

---

[1] *Politics*, I. ii. § 13.   [2] *Ethic. Nich.*, I. ii. 8.
[3] Ibid., III. ix. § 6, § 12.   [4] Ibid., VIII. i. 1.
[5] *Politics*, I. ii. § 16.

Men lived for the State. The virtue of patriotism was the primary, all-absorbing virtue of society. For this men were disposed to be frugal and industrious, prudent and just and temperate, and willing to make many sacrifices, even the sacrifice of life itself. Hence it is that Aristotle makes justice the primary virtue. "Justice," says he, "is the bond of men in States, and the administration of justice, which is the determination of what is just, is the principle of order in political society."[1] "That which is for the common interest of all is said to be just."[2] The exclusive practice of such virtues tended to make men sturdy, proud, and self-sufficient. "For," says Aristotle, "what each thing is when fully developed, we call its nature, whether we are speaking of a man, a horse, or a family. Moreover, the final cause and end of a thing is the best, and to be self-sufficing is the end and the best."[3] And this sense of self-sufficiency is the characteristic trait that runs through the story of the great heroes of antiquity. It taught revenge, but it could not teach meekness; it inculcated pride, but it could not inculcate charity.

Not but that with time, and thought, and the advance of civilization, with its increase of humanizing influences, the moral sense grew more delicate and the finer virtues came to be appreciated. Stoicism restored the link of

---

[1] *Ethic. Nich.*, X. ix. § 9.   [2] *Ibid.*, VIII. ix. § 4.
[3] *Politics*, I. ii. § 9.

union and intimacy with the Divinity, which Aristotle had missed, and in consequence established a high and unbending code of morality; but the code of Stoicism, as well indeed as all other Pagan codes of morality, was confined to a favoured few who had the leisure for meditation and aspirations and sentiments above their fellow-men. There is not a moral law of our nature that human reason is not competent to evolve. There is not a moral precept inculcated in the Gospel that had not been practised among the disciples of Pythagoras or Gautama, by Jew or Brahmin. This is the great merit of the New Law that it only elevated and sanctified and brought home to the lowliest the best and noblest aspirations of the choice souls of humanity. The evolution of the moral sense from the days of Aristotle to those of Cicero is marked. Already do we begin to hear words of sympathy for the slave, and the feeling of a universal brotherhood is dawning.[1] There are certain privileged spots near the statues of the gods in which the slave fleeing the wrath of a harsh master may find sanctuary.[2] To the moral views of Seneca and Epictetus and Marcus Aurelius the evolution is still more wonderful. Seneca is profoundly impressed with the sense of human sinfulness. He enters into himself, and makes that daily examination of his conscience which has so edified Roger Bacon.[3] "We

---

[1] Cicero, *De Officiis*, III. 6.
[2] Seneca, *De Clem.*, I. 18, vol. ii. p. 26.
[3] *Opus Tertium*, p. 306.

have all sinned," he tells us; "some more gravely, others more lightly; some from purpose, others by chance impulse, or else carried away by wickedness external to them; others of us have wanted fortitude to stand by our resolutions, and have lost our innocence unwillingly and not without a struggle."[1] But withal Seneca wavered as regards belief in a future existence. He regarded the sage as superior to God in all else but immortality. His philosophy was the philosophy of a strong nerve. Epictetus, the crippled slave who sought to make of his whole life a hymn of praise to God, is one of the noblest and most beautiful characters of antiquity.[2] He had great delicacy of conscience. He guarded his thoughts as carefully as his deeds. He also felt oppressed by the sense of sin. He asks: "Is it possible for a man to be sinless? It cannot be; but it is possible to strive unceasingly after sinlessness."[3] But Epictetus looked to no life beyond the present. Marcus Aurelius has left on record thoughts beautiful as they are consoling on nearly every aspect of morality. He was translated as a book for spiritual reading, by Cardinal Barberini, who dedicated it to his own soul in order to make it

---

[1] *De Clem.*, I. 6.

[2] As an instance of the Christian spirit of his philosophy, we cite the following :—" If any one has spoken evil of you, do not attempt to defend yourself, but simply reply : ' He who said that of me, knew not my other defects ' " (*Dissert.*, iv. cap. 12).

[3] *Dissert.*, iv. 12, § 9, vol. i. p. 667.

redder than the purple he wore at the sight of this Gentile's virtues.[1] But Marcus Aurelius never rose to a true conception of the sacredness and dignity of human life. He could not overcome Stoic indifference to suicide.

These men represent what was best in Pagan morality. But we of to-day, in the light of Christian truth and in the presence of the Sermon on the Mount, feel the shortcomings of their greatest and best codes. Stoic calm is not Christian resignation. The suppression of the affections is not their sanctification. And thus is there a profound abyss between what is highest and best in Pagan morals and the simplest practices of Christian teachings. Moreover, the sublime maxims of those choice spirits were within the reach of the cultured and leisurely few, and had little or no influence upon the many. Not that among the people of the Roman world a more humane disposition was not becoming felt. "When," says Aubé, "Alexander Severus reduced the rights of fathers over children to simple corrections; when Hadrian decreed that in future should a master be killed by his slaves the penalty of death would extend only to those surrounding his person and who might have foreseen and prevented the danger; when, going still further, he completely deprived masters of the right of life and death over their slaves—these emperors only incorporated into the laws

[1] Crossly, *Marcus Aurelius*, bk. iv., Preface, p. xix.

what was already a thing of custom."[1] All this while Christian truths and Christian maxims were dawning upon the world, and were proclaimed from forum and amphitheatre, and conviction of their truth was sealed with the blood of martyrs; and though Pagan philosophy may not have recognized the source, it could not have ignored the light that was increasing from dusk to noonday brilliancy.

We would here call attention to what we consider a confusion of language in a clever writer of the day. He says: "There are certain ages in which the sense of virtue has been the mainspring of religion; there are other ages in which this position is occupied by the sense of sin. Now, of all systems the world has ever seen, the philosophers of ancient Greece and Rome appealed most strongly to the sense of virtue, and Christianity to the sense of sin."[2] In this passage are the recognition and the misapprehension of an important truth. There

---

[1] St. Justin, *Philosophe et Martyr, Etude Critique*, Introd. p. lxx.

[2] W. H. Lecky, *Rationalism in Europe*, vol. i. pp. 388, 389. Elsewhere the author even goes farther and speaks of Pagans as holding for their ideal the beauty of holiness! "The eye of the pagan philosopher was ever fixed upon virtue, the eye of the Christian teacher upon sin. The first sought to amend men by extolling the beauty of holiness, the second by awaking the sentiment of remorse" (*European Morals*, vol. ii. p. 4). Surely, outside of a few stray expressions in Persius and other Stoics, there is nothing in Pagan literature to justify such a statement.

never was a religion without a sense of sin. This is the meaning of an altar and a sacrifice. But in the philosophies, and in the public life of ancient Greece and Rome, this sense of sin became buried out of sight among the passions and aspirations of the hour, and so naught is heard of it. The pages of Plutarch, it is true, reveal virtuous act and virtuous word, but rather as the result of a certain active energy, imparting a healthy tone to the whole man, than as deliberate deeds performed with the deliberate purpose of attaining the ends of virtue. This is not the sense of virtue. The Apollo of Belvidere is the Grecian ideal of manly grace and beauty. But what is the predominant expression? Is it not that of a proud, self-sufficient, self-reliant, well-developed, sensuous manhood, trained to the full top of its capacity? In no trait may we read the sense of virtue. We have found the later Stoic moralists fully realizing the sense of sin. But they were exceptions. To the Church is it due to have revived that almost forgotten sense, and sanctified it and made it productive of repentance, by bringing it into intimate relation with the sorrows and sufferings of the Divine Redeemer. Now, repentance means not only a rising out of sin, but also a striving after the opposite virtue.

And here is where the Divine mission of the Church becomes so apparent. She brings home to man his origin and his destiny. She instils into him that whatever there is of good in his nature, is given him for the purpose of attaining that end. Virtue is the habitual action—or rather the sum of habitual actions—tending to the end for which man was created. That end, she does not hold with Aristotle to be self-development, or self-sufficiency, or the good of the State. That end is none other than God. His Will defines the rectitude of action in which the soul should dwell. Anything that turns man away from his final destiny—anything that absorbs his attention and his energies to the total exclusion of that destiny—becomes sinful.[1] Sin, then, is the state of a soul voluntarily and freely and with open eyes, knowing what it does, diverging from its final end, which is God, putting in the stead the lesser goods of life, and making unto itself a law of its own.[2] The Church brings home to her children the great unreasonableness, injustice, and enormity of this mode of acting and living, by impressing upon them the truths that thereto is to be ascribed the whole degradation of humanity; that therefor did Jesus Christ suffer and die, in order to raise man up from the low state in which he lay prone and helpless. Therefore is it that the sense of sin is deep in the Christian heart; but there is none the less the sense of virtue, or rather the consciousness of striving after perfection by the way of virtue.

[1] *Summa Theol.*, I. i. quæst. lxiii. art. i. c.
[2] Ibid. quæst. civ. art. i. c.; I. ii. lxxi. vi.; I. ii. cix. iv. c.

The Pagan ideal was that of harmonious development of soul and body. The Christian ideal looks farther. It goes beyond the natural order. It tells us to be perfect as our Father in heaven is perfect.[1] Besides the natural virtues, it recognizes others which are of the supernatural order. There are the theological virtues of Faith in God and the truths of His Revealed Religion; of Hope for union with Him in eternity; of Charity, wherewith we love Him with all our heart and all our soul, and in Him and for Him, our neighbour as ourselves. It made predominant a criterion of excellence other than the approval of men. We catch glimpses of such a criterion in the advanced Stoics. Marcus Aurelius touched upon it when he said: "Never forget that it is possible to be at once a Divine man, yet a man unknown to all the world."[2] It is the criterion that seeks approval of God rather than of men, and cultivates the hidden virtues rather than those that shine. Christ gave the example of them in His life, and taught them in His preaching. Modesty of demeanour and humility in thought and act arising from a sense of one's unworthiness before God; chastity in thought as well as in speech and deed; obedience to all lawfully constituted authority, seeing its source and sanction in God; poverty in spirit; resignation to the Divine Will under all trials and troubles, accepting as from the Hand of God, whatever

---

[1] Matt. v. 48.   [2] *Thoughts*, vii. 67.

of sickness, or pain, or bodily infirmity, or annoyance from without that may befall one; the meekness that resents not injuries, that considers itself blessed amid revilings and persecutions, that returns good for evil; the spirit of prayer : these are a few out of the many virtues that Christianity in an especial degree made its own. These constitute the Christian ideal. It is the ideal that an Aquinas followed when, resisting the importunities of flesh and blood, he abandoned the comforts of a lordly home, that he might, in the retirement of the cloister, practice those virtues and live in intimate union with God. It is the ideal that the tens of thousands of delicate virgins, thronging the convents the world over, have in view, in entering with a light heart and a cheerful spirit upon their lives of prayer and self-devotion; it is the ideal that moulds the Sister of Charity ministering to want and disease and crime and misery. It is the ideal of Jesus and His Virgin-Mother. Here is a whole world of action and motive entirely unknown to Aristotle.

It need no longer surprise that St. Thomas surpasses himself in that portion of his masterpiece treating of morals. We stand at the sublime source whence he drew his best inspirations. Aristotle found in the State his chief reason for the practice of virtue. Indeed, he expressly tells us that "women and children must be educated with an eye to the State, if the virtues of either of them are supposed to make any difference in the virtues of the State."[1] St. Thomas regards things in the light in which the Church places them for his apprehension. That light goes beyond the convenience of State; it looks further than the gratification of human selfishness; and in doing so, it has benefited both the State and the individual. Dwell a moment upon the line of reasoning which the Church has held from the beginning. God is Creator. He is more; He is Preserver. Without His conservative act all things would fall back to their original nothingness. As air retains the light of the sun, without being itself the sun, so every creature of God participates in the being of God without sharing His Divine essence.[2] Therefore man is indebted to God not only for existence, but also for the prolonging of that existence. God created all things for Himself. He imposed upon them the law according to which they may reach their final destiny. To man has he given a rational soul by which to know the laws of his nature and to follow the path in which is traced his destiny. Hence that submission to God's law which man, in common with all other creatures, is clearly bound to pay. Hence man's responsibility toward God; hence that sense of duty; hence that voice of conscience. Again, man is endowed with a free will. God claims from him a willing homage or none at all. There is open to him the way of virtue or the way of vice. He has inbred in his nature passions which are

---

[1] *Politics*, I. iv. § 15.   [2] *Summa*, I. i. quæst. civ. art. i.

not in themselves bad, and which, when controlled, may become the means of his sanctification and perfection. Love is the source whence they all arise.[1] Love is also the principle by which they are held in hand. It is the law of union binding man with man and man with God. "He that abideth in charity, abideth in God, and God in him."[2] It is the inspiration of zeal for all good.[3] It is the principle of activity in every intellectual being. It underlies all man's actions.[4] It is the fulfilment of the law.[5] It is of God's own essence, for God is Love.

Hitherto other principles—now of might, now of right, now of justice, now of expediency—ruled men. The Gospel introduces the law of love, and before its brilliancy all other systems pale; gradually it takes possession of the public conscience, and the predominant principles of other days drop out to be imbedded in the records of history. It revolutionizes life and thought. It brings home to men, as no philosophy could ever bring home to them, the Divine lesson of an universal brotherhood based upon the mystery of redemption. It causes men to realize the sacredness of human personality. It breaks down the barriers of rank and class. It teaches the

---

[1] St. Augustine, *De Civ. Dei*, lib. xiv. cap. 7, 9.
[2] 1 John iv. 16.
[3] *Summa*, I. ii. quæst. xxvi. art ii.
[4] "Manifestum est quod omne agens, quodcumque sit, agit quamcumque actionem ex aliquo amore" (ibid., I. ii. quæst. xxviii. art. vi.).
[5] Romans xiii. 10.

doctrine of true liberty, true equality, and true fraternity. It looks upon the soul of a slave as something as precious in the sight of God as that of a free-born citizen. It inculcates the dignity of labour. The Pagan world understood the value of labour, but the Pagan world never raised itself up to a proper conception of the dignity of labour. Labour had become so identified with slavery that it was considered degrading. The artisan was unfit to be a citizen. He was too busy to practise virtue. "No man," says Aristotle, "living the life of a mechanic or labourer, can practise virtue."[1] All this was changed by Jesus, the Son of the carpenter.[2] He blessed the poor. He raised up and dignified labour. He showed men how to sanctify it. And so, that which had been regarded as a curse and a hardship, has come to be the greatest blessing to man, to soothe his pains, to heal the wounds of a troubled heart, to develop energy, and to help him to save his soul. Pagan legislation taught men how to endure privations and sufferings for their country's sake; it taught them to see naught of good beyond the narrow limits of their own territory; it inspired them with no sympathy for weakness, no consolation for sorrow, no reverence for old age, no tenderness for decrepitude, no sense of the awful sanctity of human life. It exposed the helpless weakling as unfit to live;[3] it sanctioned

---

[1] *Politics*, III. v. § 5.   [2] Luke iv. 22.
[3] Labourt, *Recherches Historiques sur les Enfants Trouvés*, pp. 11 *seq*. Paris, 1845.

and at times commanded the destruction of the babe yet unborn;[1] it placed in the hands of the head of the household, the power of life and death over slave, wife, and child.[2] All this, with more equally criminal and equally unjust, had been of ancient law and ancient custom. It has passed out of the public conscience. A new law, the Law of Divine Love and Divine Grace, shines upon the world and renews the face of the earth.

[1] Aristotle, *Politics*, VII. xvi. § 10.
[2] Laws of Solon. See Labourt, ibid., p. 16; Troplong, *De l'Influence du Christianisme sur le Droit civil des Romains*, p. 314.

XIII.

CONCLUSION.

THIS outline will enable us to form some conception of the relations of Aristotle to the Christian Church. Let us review those relations from our present vantage-ground. A great philosopher comes among men. He reduces thought and the expression of thought to a science. He teaches the secret of method; he shows how to define and to divide; he initiates into the mode of observing and classifying the facts of nature, and of constructing the natural sciences. The wonderful grasp of his genius takes hold of the human intellect in the East and in the West, and marks out for it the grooves in which it shall think and the very terms and forms of expression it shall use for all time. Other geniuses may charm the human intellect, and be suggestive of thought and systems of thought, but it is only Aristotle who has been able to impose upon humanity his very forms of thought and expression to that extent that they are to-day as much part of our thinking as the idioms of our speech. And there is no department of human science to which his dominion does not extend. His least hint runs along lines of study age after age till we find it finally blossoming into some great discovery. He states, for instance, that this world is not very large; that there is only one sea between the country at the Pillars of Hercules and India; and that communication between their coasts is neither incredible nor impossible.[1] That stray remark is transmitted down the ages until it falls into the hands of a Columbus, and forthwith it shapes his destiny and leads to the finding of a new world. Here is how Columbus speaks: "Aristotle says that this world is small, that there is little water, and that one could easily pass from Spain into Media. Avouruyz[2] confirms this idea, and Cardinal Peter d'Aliaco[3] cites it, supporting this opinion, which is conformable to that of Seneca, by saying that Aristotle might know many secret things of this world on account of Alexander the Great."[4] Thus it is that even America cannot be discovered without having connected with it the name of Aristotle.

The Church, in her mission of renovating the world and raising it up into a higher plane of thought and action, makes use of the human instruments at her command. She is not exclusive. Her activity extends to all classes—to the ignorant and the learned, to the

---

[1] *De Cælo*, lib. ii. cap. xiv. 15.
[2] Averroës. [3] Peter d'Ailly.
[4] See C. Jourdain, *De l'Influence d'Aristote et de ses Interprètes sur la découverte du Nouveau-Monde*, p. 29. Paris, 1861.

rich and the poor. To each does she speak in the language each best understands. And in speaking to the human intelligence, she has made use of that language most clearly expressed by the human intelligence, and has drawn from that philosophy which has left the most profound impress upon human thought. In her teachings concerning the sacraments she has applied the Aristotelian doctrine of Matter and Form, of Substance and Accidence. In her moral and intellectual philosophy, when speaking of the human soul and its faculties, of virtues and vices, of habits and passions, she has adopted Aristotle's definitions and divisions of subjects. And thus has the language of this Pagan philosopher become the medium by which the most sacred teachings and the most awful mysteries of the Church are conveyed to the human understanding. Nor would Aristotle take amiss this use of his writings. He realized the sacred ministry of philosophy. He considered it the most Divine and the most elevated of all subjects, since it treats of God and of things Divine; "for," he adds, "according to the avowal of the whole human race, God is the Cause and Principle of Things."[1]

Indeed, it is noteworthy in those days of secularization, when men in all departments of science seek to do without God, even to the ignoring of His very existence, how scrupulously the Pagan philosopher, in all his

[1] *Metaphysics*, II. ii. § 20.

studies, keeps ever in mind the Divinity. Is he dealing with first principles of science and thought? As the crowning-point of his speculations, back of all elementary truths, he discerns and acknowledges the Living Truth Who is their source.[1] Is he contemplating the starry heavens? He reads in their motion, as clearly as the Psalmist ever read, the resplendent glory of their Prime-Mover. God is the end for which they exist; He is the Life of all life, the Mover of all motion, and the Eternal Source of all time.[2] Is he fathoming the problems of time and space, of motion and rest, of the finite and the infinite? Again, in his gropings after light, through the mists of those obscure questionings, rays of the Divinity penetrate, and he clearly recognizes the Being Who is without parts, indivisible, without magnitude, immeasurable; he finds God.[3] Is he investigating the wonders of the animal kingdom? He does so with an enthusiasm and a reverence that raise him above whatever may seem offensive or loathsome to the senses. In the formation, the design and the function of the least organ, he reads somewhat of the power and the beauty of Nature. Throughout the whole domain of animal life he finds no place for chance. Every organ has its purpose. From the contemplation of the fitness and harmony which he perceives in all parts of the animal kingdom, he ascends

[1] *Met.*, XII., cap. vii., viii. [2] *De Cœlo*, lib. i. cap. ix.
[3] *Naturales Auscultationes*, lib. viii. cap. xv. 6.

to the Divinity that determines their various functions.[1] Be the subject of his studies what it may, it invariably ends in a hymn of praise to the Godhead. Surely, modern thinkers might well hesitate before censuring a religious attitude of mind constantly practised by the greatest intellect of antiquity.

But the philosophy that the Church has sanctioned—the philosophy of the Schools as expressed by their greatest and most representative genius, St. Thomas Aquinas—is a far different system of philosophy from that enunciated by the Stagyrite. It accepts from him his methods, his definitions, his terms, whatever is conformable to the Divine teachings, and it supplements them with other truths and other conceptions of truth more in consonance with the Divine mission of the Church. It is deeply rooted in the Early Fathers and in the decrees of the Councils. The outward form is Aristotelian, but the inner spirit is that of Christianity. It is this spirit that gives it life and power and extends its influence far beyond the domain of technical language. It is by reason of this spirit, that, to use the words of another, "Christian philosophy is the basis of our social existence; it nourishes the roots of our laws, and by it do we live far more than by ideas saved from the wreck of the Greek and Roman world."[2] The Church makes

[1] *De Partibus Animalium*, lib. i. cap. v.
[2] Troplong, *De l'Influence du Christianisme sur le Droit Civil des Romains*, p. 364. Paris, 1843.

use of speculation only so far as it is essential to ground her doctrines and her practices in human reason. But it is not by means of speculation that she has renewed the face of the earth. It is rather by the seeds of Faith, which she has sown, and which have given forth a rich harvest of zeal, devotion, sanctity, and the edifying practice of every virtue. Philosophy is cold comfort under affliction, or want, or misery, or in the face of a great calamity. That which was best amongst the Stoics—the philosophy of Marcus Aurelius—was only a tonic bracing up the whole man to meet death or anticipate its coming by suicide. It taught the resignation of despair. That which is most probing among the moderns—the philosophy of Schopenhauer—finds nothing in life worth living for, and has consolation only for the man who is disgusted with living and resolved upon terminating his own career. It also teaches resignation, but it is likewise the resignation of despair. And Christianity inculcates resignation, but it is the resignation of love, and hope, and faith, awaiting the future, and knowing that all things are in the hands of a Divine Father. The one is the resignation of death; the other is a life-giving, active, hopeful, and saving resignation. Philosophy may speculate; Christianity acts. Speculation may console a few philosophers of leisure; but the soothing hand of Christian charity, nerved by the love of God and the love of man, and the consoling voice of Religion, moved by the spirit of Faith, can alone revive expiring hopes, strengthen wavering resolutions for good, bring calm to the troubled mind, raise a soul out of despondency, and cause man to suffer and endure in a prayerful spirit all the pain that life may bring, knowing that in so doing he is best securing his individual perfection and sanctification, and best fulfilling the end for which he was created.

APPENDIX.

We here give the full text of the important letter of Gregory IX., appointing a commission to examine and expurge the prohibited books of Aristotle. That the W in the letter stands for William of Auxerre, is confirmed beyond a shadow of doubt by the other letters of Gregory to the King and Queen of France, quoted by Du Boulay (*Historia Universitatis Parisiensis*, tom. iii. p. 145), in which the name—*Willielmum Antissiodorensem*—is given in full. It will be noticed that Gregory makes use of a Scriptural allusion which is a favourite one with both Jerome and Origen when impressing the necessity of studying secular letters. The original document is in the Bibliothéque Nationale (Suppl. lat. num., 1575), where it was brought to light by M. La Porte du Theil, and transcribed by M. Hauréau into the *Notices et Extraits des Manuscrits*, tom. xxi. partie ii. p. 222.

"Gregorius, &c., &c., magistris W. archdiacono Belvacensi, Symoni de Auteis, Ambianensi, et St. de Pruvino, Remensi, canonicis.

"Cum sapientiæ sacræ paginæ reliquæ scientiæ debeant famulari, eatenus sunt a fidelibus amplectendæ quatenus obsequi dinoscuntur beneplacitis dominantis, ut si quid in eis fuerit virulentum, vel aliter vitiosum, quod derogare possit fidei puritati, eminus respuatur: quia inventa in

"Gregory, &c., &c., to W. Archdeacon of Beauvais, Symon of Authie, Canon of Amiens, and Stephen of Provins, Canon of Rheims.

"As other sciences ought to minister to the wisdom of Holy Writ, the Faithful should embrace them according as they perceive them giving willing service to the sovereign master; so that should aught of poison or other vicious thing be found in them calculated to diminish

numero captivorum mulier speciosa, non aliter in domum permittitur introduci, nisi rasa superfluitatis cæsarie, ac unguibus lacerantibus circumcisis; et, ut spoliatis Ægyptiis ditentur Hebræi, jubentur vasa aurea et argentea pretiosa, non æruginosa, ænea, vel lignea, mutuari. Ceterum cum, sicut intelleximus, libri Naturalium, qui Parisiis in concilio provinciali fuere prohibiti, quædam utilia et inutilia continere dicantur, ne utile per inutile vitietur, discretioni vestræ, de qua plenam in Domino fiduciam obtinemus, per apostolica scripta, sub obtestatione divini judicii, firmiter præcipiendo mandamus, quatenus libros ipsos examinantes, sicut convenit, subtiliter et prudenter, quæ ibi erronea, seu scandali, vel offendiculi, legentibus inveneritis illata ava, penitus resecetis, ut, quæ sunt suspecta remotis, incunctanter ac inoffense in reliquis studeatur.

"Datum Laterani, ix. Cal. Maii, pontificatus nostri anno quinto."

the purity of the Faith, the same should be cast far away. Thus the beautiful woman found among the captives was not permitted to be brought into the house till her hair was shaven and her nails were cut. Thus, that the Hebrews might grow rich with the spoils of the Egyptians, they were commanded to borrow their precious vases of gold and silver, leaving aside those of brass, copper, or wood. Having learned, then, that certain books of natural philosophy, which were prohibited by the Provincial Council of Paris, are said to contain things useful and baneful, and lest the baneful should mar the useful, We strongly enjoin upon your discretion, in which We place full confidence, by these Apostolic letters, under invocation of the Divine judgment, to examine those books with as minute care and prudence as behove, and to remove whatever is erroneous, or of scandal, or in the least offensive to the readers, so that after the severe pruning of all suspected passages, what remains, may, without delay and without danger, be restored to study.

"Given at the Lateran, April 23, and the fifth year of our Pontificate."

INDEX.

A

Abelard, 23
Abraham of Casca, 30
Abubacer, 45
Adelard of Bath, 24
Agapetus, Pope, 31
Agnostic, the, 81
Albert the Great, 42, 43, 66, 86–89
Alcuin, 11, 23
Alexander the Great, 13, 129
Alexander IV., 68
Alexander of Hales, 74, 91
Alexander Severus, 118
Alexandrian School, 4, 6
Al-Farabi, 35, 42
Al-Gazali, 43
Alhambra, 50
Al-Kendi, 35
Al-Makkari, quoted, 35
Al-Mamoun, 35
Al-Mótawakkel, 35
Amaury of Bennes, 51, 74
Anselm of Laon, 24
Anselm, St., 23
Antioch, School of, 28
Apologists, 7
Appollinarius, 28
Arabian numbers, 34
Aristotle, his genius, 16
——, his writings and influence, 13-17
Aristotle, his works translated into Syriac, 29, 30
—— on the problem of knowing, 39
——, a list of his works studied in the University of Paris, 68
——, his conception of God, 100
——, his conception of the soul, 107
——, his definition of the soul, 108
—— on happiness, 113
——, his theory of morals, 114, 115
——, his remarks encourage Columbus, 129
—— on the ministry of Philosophy, 130
—— finds God in all his studies 131
Aristotelian logic, 12
Artemon, 27
Athenagoras, 8
Athens, 12
Aubé on amelioration of Roman law, 118
Augustine, the Church's influence over him, 3
—— bases his teachings on the Nicene Creed, 11
—— on the use of philosophy, 97
Avempace, 35, 44
Averroës mentioned by Columbus, 129

Index.

Averroës on the universal soul, 41
——, his Commentaries, 47
Averroistic doctrines, 71, 72, 77
Avicenna, 35
—— and scholastic philosophy, 43

B

Bacon, Francis, 14, 92
Bacon, Roger, 67
——, the spirit in which he worked, 91
——, on experiment, 92, 93
——, on bad translations of Aristotle, 93
Bagdad, School of, 31
Barberini, Cardinal, on Marcus Aurelius, 117
Bardesanes, 28
Bar-Gilân, John, 42
Bec, Monastery of, 23
Beda, 23
Bernard the Sub-Deacon, 52
Bibliothèque Nationale, 135
Boëthius, 12
——, his translations of Aristotle, 18, 19
Bonaventura, 73
Brahmin, 116
Brescian, John, 67
Brewer, Professor, on the Schoolmen, 96

C

Cambridge, 54
Cassiodorus, 22, 31
Catechism uses philosophical language, 2
Charlemagne, 11
Christian Schools of Alexandria, 9
Church, attitude of, towards philosophy, 1–6
—— not a school of philosophy, 1
Clement of Alexandria, 9

Clement the Hibernian, 11
Columbus, 129
Councils of the Church, 97
Cousin, 15
Cumas, 29

D

Darwin, Charles, 91
David of Dinant, 52, 74
Descartes, 14
Dialectics taught up to eleventh century, 23
Diaphantus, 34
Diodorus of Tarsus, 28
Dionysian writings, 11, 12
Du Boulay on the University of Paris, 65

E

Early Fathers, the, 97
Edessa, School of, 28–30
Emanated intellect, 41
Empedocles, 39
Ephraim, St., his genius and influence, 29
Epictetus, 117
Eternal Gospel, the, 51, 73
Eudes, Chancellor, 67
Eusebius, 27

F

Friends of God, Society of, 12

G

Galen, 34
Gautama, 116
Genus and Species, the problem of, 19
Gilles, Brother, 71
Gnosticism, 6, 38
Gregory Nazianzen, 27
Gregory the Great, 22

Gregory IX., 56
——, his character, 58
—— on Michael Scott, 60
——, his letter authorizing the revision of Aristotle, 135

H

Hampden quoted, 102, 112
Hannan, 31
Hasan, 37
Hauréau quoted, 42, 49, 66, 75, 86
Hayy ibn-Yakdhân, 54
Hegel, 15, 81
Hellenic culture, 5
Hellenism kept alive by Irish monks, 11, 12
Hindu, 34
Hobaish, 31
Honain, 31
Humanists, 14

I

Ibas, 29
Ibn-Habib of Seville, 35
Ibn-Khakan, 35
Ibn-Roschd—*Averroës*, 35, 46
Ibn-Sina—*Avicenna*, 43
Ibn-Tofaïl—*Abubacer*, 42
Innocent III., 55, 56
Irenæus, 26
Irish monks, influence of, 11, 12
Isaac, son of Honain, 31
'Isa ben-Ya'hya, 43
Isidore of Seville, 23

J

Jerome, St., 28
John of Damascus, 11, 25, 27
John of Salisbury, 20, 50
John the Evangelist, 5
Justin Martyr, 7, 8

K

Kadrites, 37
Kant, 15
Kilwardby, Robert, 73
Korân, the, 34, 36, 38

L

Labour dignified by Christianity, 126
—— sanctified by Jesus, 126
Lanfranc, 23
Langton, Stephen, 59
La Porte du Theil, 135
Lecky on the Church popularizing philosophic truth, 2, 3
—— on the sense of sin and the sense of virtue, 119, 120
Legislation, pagan, its shortcomings, 126, 127
Leo XIII. on St. Thomas Aquinas, 99
Limitations of thought, 79
Love, law of, 2
—— the source of all passion, 125
—— the fulfilment of the law, 125
Lucian, St., 28
Luther on Aristotle, 14

M

Maimonides, 42
Makrizi, quoted, 36
Marcus Aurelius, 117, 122, 133
Maximus, St., and the Dionysian writings, 11
Mill, J. S., 15
Mohammedanism, 96
Motazales, doctrine of, 38
Motécallamin, 37
Mullinger, J. Bass, on the University of Paris, 53
Munk quoted, 43
Mussulman philosophy, 33
Mysticism, 12

N

Narses, 30
Nazareth, 81
Neo-Platonism, 11, 55, 77
Nestorians cultivate Aristotle, 27
Newman and the Church, 3
Nicæa, Council of, 10
Nicene Creed, 10
Nisibus, 29, 30, 31
Novalis and the Church, 3

O

Origen, 9, 10
Original sin, 104
Oxford, 54, 73

P

Paris, Provincial Council of, 53
———, University of, 50
Parthenon, 50
Paul of Samosata, 27
Paul, St., compares Christianity with Hellenic culture, 5
Personality, doctrine of, 102, 103
Peter d'Ailly, 129
Peter the Lombard, 24
Philip de Grève, 57, 66
Philo, 4, 5
Plato and Aristotle, 16, 17
———, false writings of, 39
Plotinus, 11
Pontus, Council of, 27
Porphyry, 12, 19, 20
Pouchet on Albert the Great and Roger Bacon, 93
Principles ruling in morality, 125
Probus, 29
Proclus, 11
Pythagoras, 39, 116

R

Raimund, 67
Raymond of Toledo, 49
Reason fallible, 83
Robert of Courçon, 56
Roscellin, 23
Rosmini, 21

S

Schlegel, F., and the Church, 3
Schoolmen, the, 77
Schopenhauer, 15, 81, 133
Scott, Michael, 59 60, 65, 91
Scotus Erigena, 12
Seneca, 117
Simeon Beth-Arsam, 30
Simeon the Just, 39
Simon of Authie, 62
Sister of Charity, her ideal, 123
Source of Science, 27
Summa Theologica, 100
Spencer, Herbert, 15
Spirit of Faith, 82
State, the, in Aristotle's Ethics, 114
Stephen of Provins, 63
Stoics, 133
Suso, Henry, 12

T

Tauler, 12
Tempier, Stephen, 71
Tertullian, 8
Theodore of Mopsuesta, 29
Theology of Aristotle, apocryphal, 40
Thomas Aquinas, St., and Averroës, 47
———, called to Rome, 70
———, recalled to Paris, 72
———, the spirit in which he worked, 89

——, prepares a treatise on engineering, 94
——, on creation, 106
——, on the soul, 109
——, on the problem of knowing, 110, 111
Thomas Aquinas, St., his ideal, 123
Tiraboschi on Urban IV., 70
Toledo, Academy of, 49
Town and Gown, 63
Triumph of St. Thomas, by Traini, 95, 96

U

Urban IV., 69
—— calls Aquinas to Rome, 70
Urban V. installs Aristotle in the University of Paris, 74

V

Vacherot on Christianity, 4
Vienne, Council of, 108
Vincent of Beauvais, 42

W

Wacel ben-'Atha, 37
Wilhelmina, the Beguin, 74
William d'Aire, 52
William of Auvergne, 42
William of Auxerre, 61, 135
William of Moerbek, 47

THE END.

PRINTED BY WILLIAM CLOWES AND SONS, LIMITED, LONDON AND BECCLES.

www.ingramcontent.com/pod-product-compliance
Lightning Source LLC
Chambersburg PA
CBHW030352170426
43202CB00010B/1347